Hollow Victory

how to **Identify & Disarm** **5 Landmines** that make **Victorious Christian Living Feel Like A Lie**

What Others Are Saying About Hollow Victory...

"Too many Christians are frustrated with the chasm between the truth of God's word and the reality of their own emotional struggles. Tara Johnson has written a sensitive but hard-hitting book that builds a bridge across that divide. She is not just preaching in these pages. She has lived this stuff and that is why her book is so refreshing and powerful."

NathanSakany
Incubator Creative Group

'Hollow Victory *tackles the difficult subjects that many Christians try to avoid. Tara writes honestly, sincerely, and with a healthy dose of humor. Her habitual truthfulness is refreshing and invigorating.*"

Elizabeth Medlock

"This book is a great resource to help in healing. Tara shares her heart and her own real-life struggles. The challenge of self discovery can be tough but it is so worth the trip... and Tara is a terrific guide on the pathway."

Kathy Vernich

"I want a lot of copies of Hollow Victory *to share with my family and friends. I just had to keep reading. I couldn't stand the wait to finish it!"*

Pastor Steve Shepherd

"If you only read one book this year, make sure it is Hollow Victory. *Tara Johnson has a heart for God and a passion for helping hurting people. Her honesty and compassion are clearly evident in her writing. What are you waiting for? Time with Tara will bring healing to your soul — and there is no better way to spend time with her than reading* Hollow Victory.*"*

Tami Rowbotham
MyMinistryCafe.com

Hollow Victory

how to **Identify & Disarm** **5 Landmines** that make **Victorious Christian Living Feel Like A Lie**

Tara Johnson

Taylor Morgan Press

Hollow Victory: How To Identify & Disarm Five Landmines That Make Victorious Christian Living Feel Like A Lie

Copyright 2013 by Tara Johnson

All rights reserved. No part of this publication may be reproduced, stored in a retrieval system, or transmitted in any form or by any means — electronic, mechanical, photocopy, recording, or any other — except for brief quotations in printed reviews, without the prior permission of the publisher.

A Study Guide by the author is available.

Cover design by Villa Productions

Cover photo "Land mine near Bir Hacheim (1990)" by Jerryscuba at Wikimedia Commons is published under a Creative Commons Attribution-Share Alike 3.0 Unported License

Printed in the United States of America

Published by Taylor Morgan Press — Alexander, Arkansas

ISBN-1484100131

Dedication

To my Grandmother Fern Downing

A woman who experienced many of her own 'landmines' yet never lost her sense of humor, her ability to laugh or her faith in God. You are missed. You are loved. When I look up at the stars, I think of you and smile.

Contents

Acknowledgments..11
Introduction..15
Hollow Victory...25
Landmines: Where Do They Come From, Anyway? 31
Landmine #1: Grief...41
   Grief Section 2: December's Songbird 45
   Grief Section 3: But Don't Take My Word For It.........49
   Grief Section 4: Developing A 20/20 Perspective........57
   Grief Section 5: Rainbows and Rain............................69
Landmine #2: Depression...73
   Depression Section 2: Finding Summertime Again......81
   Depression Section 3: Being The Hands Of Jesus........87
   Depression Section 4: But Don't Take My Word For It......91
   Depression Section 5: A Special Look at Pastors and Depression....113
Landmine #3 : Perfectionism..127
   Perfectionism Section 2: How God Sees Us................139
   Perfectionism Section 3: Godly Imperfectionism In Action....147
Landmine # 4: People Pleasing (All Door Mats Enter Here!)....153
   People Pleasing Section 2: Why We Wear The Mask....161
   People Pleasing Section 3: From Doormat To Tapestry....169
   People-Pleasing Section 4: Don't Take My Word For It....179
Landmine # 5: Fear and Anxiety...189
   Fear and Anxiety Section 2: Shaking From The Inside Out....193
   Fear and Anxiety Section 3: Panic Attacks.................203
   Fear and Anxiety Section 4: Giantaphobia..................209
Embracing Healing and Transformation................................215
   Healing and Transformation Section 2: Understanding Grace....223
   Healing and Transformation Section 3: A Date with Jesus....229
   Healing and Transformation Section 4: Speaking and Listening....239
Conclusion: Dancing in Victory..247
Appendix: First Things First..251
References..255
About The Author...257

Acknowledgments

Writing this book has been a lifetime dream and it is with humble thanks that I confess it could not have been possible without the amazing family and friends God has given me.

To my husband Todd and my beautiful children Bethany, Callie, Taylor, Morgan and Nathan: you make this life the most beautiful treasured gift. I can't imagine this journey without you. Your smiles, giggles and love make me the most blessed girl on the planet. Taylor and Morgan...I can't wait to meet you someday and get to rock you like I've longed to do. Mommy can't wait to love on you!

To Dad and Mom: thank you for being such an amazing example of Christ's love. To quote Natalie Grant, "God gave me your eyes, but it was you who taught me how to see". Thank you for leading me to Jesus and for all the quiet sacrifices you've made through the years.

To all my family: Ron, Linda (best in-laws ever), Brian, Courtney, Avery B, Boo-Boo, Kym, Alexa, Savannah, Bryson, Josh and Lynnley and all my extended family...our time together is the best!

To Grandma Gladys for being my biggest cheerleader and to Grandma Fern for giving me the gift of music.

To my Pilgrim Rest church family: you aren't just my 'church', you're my literal family in every sense of the word.

Thanks for your love, encouragement, friendship and joy. Serving the Lord is a pleasure with you. You are the most loving group of people I know.

To my Wednesday night teen class: thanks for keeping me on my toes! Many of the things brought out in this book are a result of studying to keep ahead of you guys. You rock! (Exclamation mark) ;)

To Dr. Snyder: thank you for letting me cry on your shoulder and showing me the path towards boundaries and freedom.

To my ministry supporters (Dad, Mom, Ron, Linda, Grandma, Gene Roebuck, Ernie & Lana Bolieu, Ed Morris, Richard & Kathy Shannon, Tony & Nancy Brown, Linda Miller, Evelyn Bruce, Jason & Brandi Glass and Pilgrim Rest MBC) and to all who have supported in the past. This ministry would not be possible without you. I love you guys!

To the awesome friends who were willing to grant me interviews: Steve, David, Bill, Ernie, Christy, Evelyn, Linda, Kathy, Kay, Bill Driggers, Cindy, Carrie, Debra, Dominic, Scott, Kerrie, Nan, Crystal, Marilyn, Janet, Kathy, Becky and the respectfully anonymous...your gift is helping so many others. Thank you!

To my unbelievable friends that make up the Incubator Chicks: Shine, Judy, Pami, Sherrie, Cori, Jackie, Jenny, Carolyn, ...and of course, Kevin. I cannot imagine this journey without you. Your love and laughter is priceless. All the chickens in the house say 'Whoop! Whoop!'

To Nate, Tami, Julie and everyone working with my awesome management team at Incubator Creative Group: you took this little fledging, insecure creature and equipped her with priceless gifts. Your love, friendship, encouragement, and yes, even the occasion kick in the pants has turned this ministry from a struggling endeavor into a blossoming and booming adventure. You guys are dream-catchers! Thank you for loving me, demonstrating wisdom and even telling me to 'Suck it up!' when needed. I'm honored to call each of you 'friend'. And an extra special thank you to Nate for pushing me farther than I thought I could go.

To Jesus, my Savior, Redeemer, Lord, Prince of Peace, Shepherd and Friend: I pledged an oath to You that anything I wrote would be for Your honor and glory, and with Your help, I intend to keep my promise. Thank you for loving me when I'm unlovable, guiding me in this journey and giving Your all for my future. Like Mary of Bethany, the purpose of my life is to live at Your feet. Empty me of myself and fill me with You. I love You...forever.

Hollow Victory · 14

INTRODUCTION

The alarm blared into Susan's ear. Amid the unwelcoming noise, she blearily cracked open an eye to stare at the blinking digital numbers. *Six o'clock already? I feel like I just went to sleep!* Her arms felt like lead. Her head felt fuzzy and her limbs refused to move. *Lord, there just isn't enough caffeine in the world to help me move today.*

It seemed like lately, no matter how much sleep she got, it was never enough. Susan rolled over to stare at the mustard colored walls of her bedroom. She despised the color, but Mike loved it. Had insisted on it. She squeezed her eyes against the yellow vision. The burnt color did nothing for her weary mood.

Mike's soft snores resounded in the room. She blew out an exhausted breath. She would be getting little help from him today. As usual, getting the kids ready for school would fall solely on her shoulders. She slowly untangled herself from the covers and stood up, feeling like she was eighty instead of thirty-five. She shuffled to the closet and eyed her clothes, sighing in disgust. Most of them were too tight. At first she thought it was the dryer, but it was getting more obvious that she was putting on weight. The mirror didn't lie and neither did the scales. How she wished they would!

Grabbing a loose fitting skirt and top that she'd worn far too frequently lately, she stumbled through her morning routine. After trying to rouse the kids for the third time, she walked slowly into the kitchen, eying the empty coffee pot. Trying to brew a pot now would be useless. It wouldn't be ready until after they left. She eyed the box of pop tarts on the counter. *No! I need to lose weight. I won't eat one no matter how convenient it is.*

After yelling up the stairs, the kids finally stumbled down and entered the kitchen, hair akimbo and eyes looking gritty.

"Good morning, guys! What would you like for breakfast?" She tried to ignore the cramp of hunger in her own stomach. The kids came first and their time was limited. Jennifer mumbled "Frosted Flakes" while Tyler opted for Pop-tarts. Guilt twisted her heart. They really needed a more nutritious breakfast but there was so little time in the morning.

While they ate, she packed lunches for the kids and Mike before eying the pile of mail he'd placed on the counter the evening before. Wincing in anticipation of what she'd find, she thumbed through the pile. Bills, bills, junk mail...she dropped the letters in disgust. Nothing good there.

She looked up at the clock. They were already five minutes behind. "Okay, kids, hurry! Brush your teeth and grab your backpacks. We've gotta go ASAP!" The kids scrambled leaving half of their breakfast behind. She eyed the dirty bowl and plate. There was no hope for it now. It would have to sit there until she came home from work.

She grabbed their lunches and her purse, and raced to the door, digging for her keys in the bottom. The kids came back down the stairs with their backpacks, pushing and shoving in sibling frustration. "Stop, you two! No arguing this morning." Jennifer unzipped her backpack and pulled out a sheet of paper.

"Hey, Mom, I forgot to tell you that the PTO needs you to make two dozen brownies for a bake sale tomorrow."

"Jennifer! Why didn't you tell me last night? Tonight is Wednesday...church, baths, homework...we barely have time to eat!"

Jennifer shrugged her slim shoulders. "Sorry, Mom, I just forgot. But remember you didn't help with the last fundraiser and you promised you would this time."

She blew out a frustrated breath. *Don't freak out. We'll just swing by Walmart on the way home. That's why it's there.* She ushered the kids out the door and mentally ran through her day's to-do list. They piled into the van and she uttered a quick prayer that it would start up with no trouble this morning. It had been acting sluggish but she hadn't told Mike yet. His temper was never good when things broke down and she didn't have the energy to deal with his moods today.

Hearing the rev of the engine, she sighed in relief and lifted up a quick prayer. *Thank you, Lord!*

She half-listened to Jennifer's happy chatter as they drove down the busy streets to school. Looking in the rearview mirror, she watched Tyler staring quietly out his window. Her son was so quiet. She constantly tried to draw him out of his shell, but he rarely shared news about school or his day. Most of the time she had to guess and imagine what went on in his seven year old world. Were all little boys like this?

She pulled up to the school and dropped the kids off. Due to traffic, they were now fifteen minutes late. *I hope the kids don't get another tardy.* She'd lost count of how many this made now. *Maybe if I started making the kids' lunches the night before, we would have enough time to get out the door earlier.*

Minutes later, she rushed into the office, shooting a look of apology at her boss. He arched an eyebrow and she gave him a tentative smile before plopping down at her desk. Most of the other employees were already hard at work, clicking away on their computers and chattering on business calls. Her stomach rumbled in protest to the morning's neglect.

It was going to be a long day.

~ ~ ~

She blinked at her glowing computer screen. All the characters were starting to run together. A throb of pain was beginning to pulse behind her eyes. Not another headache.
She leaned back and blew out a slow breath. Maybe she just needed a break. She couldn't seem to concentrate this morning. She kept having to re-read things two and three times before they even made sense. All she could concentrate on was how wonderful it would feel to crawl between her cool bed sheets tonight.

Before she could stretch, her boss strolled up. "Susan, how's it going this morning?"

Ignoring the pain throbbing in her head, she pasted on a smile. "Just fine. And you?"

He cleared his throat. "Well, uh, honestly, I'm a little concerned. I just reviewed your last report and I'm afraid I found several errors in it."

Panic slammed in her chest. "What? I checked that report three times!"

He smiled apologetically. "I know, and I'm sorry. Anyone can have an off day, Susan. Do you mind making the corrections for me?"

She hated letting people down. Biting back tears, she nodded and tried to keep control as she reached for the report. He patted her on the shoulder and left. What was wrong with her? A wave of despondency hit her in the stomach. Lately, it seemed like her best was never good enough.

Her phone rang. "Hello, Susan Daniels? This is Mrs. Johnson. Tyler's teacher at school."

Fear squeezed her heart. Was he sick? "Yes, Mrs. Johnson. Is everything okay?"

"Well, mostly. But I'm calling because I'm concerned about Tyler. He hasn't been turning in any of his homework from the past week."

Confusion furrowed her brow. She had watched Tyler doing his homework every evening. When she asked him about it, he assured her that he'd finished it. "Oh? He's been doing his work every night. Has he not turned it in?"

"I'm afraid not, Susan. And I hate to mention it, but he's been getting into lots of arguments with Cole Jenkins."

My sweet little Tyler, fighting? Surely this teacher was confused.

She continued, "Would it be alright if we scheduled a meeting to chat about this, say, this afternoon at 4:00?"

Susan bit her lip. Wednesday. Homework, baths, church, a trip to Walmart for brownies. But what else could she do? "Of course, 4:00 will be fine. See you then."

"Alright. Thank you."

She hung up and rubbed her aching head. Her stomach pinched in hunger. She opened her desk drawer and rummaged around until her fingers closed around the tube of Rolaids she kept on hand. Looking across the office, she spied the Coke machine beckoning her. She had tried giving up her Diet Cokes because the carbonation left her reflux in misery. But right now, she needed caffeine and anything that would fill up her stomach.

~ ~ ~

Lunchtime arrived and she had yet to correct her report. It seemed that every time she sat down to start, another co-worker approached needing help with their projects. She reached for another Rolaid and glared at the now empty can of Diet Coke on her desk. Maybe she should go downstairs for lunch, grab a salad and try to work through her lunch break.

Before she could move, Ruby Downs popped her head into her work space. Grinning ear to ear, she asked, "Susan? Are you ready to go?"

She stared at Ruby in blank confusion. "Ready for what?"

Ruby's sunny smile began to evaporate. "Remember? Mr. Meyers asked us to pick up the Christmas decorations for the office. Today is the only day I can do it. Are you ready?"

Had she agreed to go decoration shopping? She rubbed her head in frustration. Seems like she vaguely remembered to agreeing to help do something for Christmas but all the details had escaped. "Oh, Ruby, I'm so sorry I forgot. Today isn't looking very good. Can we do it tomorrow? Or Friday?"

Ruby shook her head. "No, it has to be today. I'm off the next two days. Roy is taking me to Branson for an early Christmas present." She giggled in an annoyingly happy fashion. The older woman seemed oblivious to Susan's stress level.

She opened her mouth to refuse but the words of Christ filled her thoughts, *"If you have done to the least of these, you have done it unto me..."* Stuffing down her frustration, she nodded and grabbed her purse. Looking back, she also grabbed the quickly disappearing pack of Rolaids.

~ ~ ~

Susan almost dropped the shopping sacks when she got back to the office and saw the clock. It was 2:00 already?

The deadline for the report was this afternoon. No breakfast. No lunch. She eyed the vending machine in the break room. Looks like it was a Snickers bar for lunch. *Oh well, I can always start my diet tomorrow...*

Licking the chocolate off her fingers, she tackled the report. Why couldn't she seem to focus? Trying to find the mistakes was like clawing her way through dried cement. When she looked up, the clock said 3:45. She only had 15 minutes to make it to the school! She stared at the report, dread spilling in her stomach. This was far from her best work. She swallowed and dropped it into her boss' correspondence box. There was nothing she could do about it now.

~ ~ ~

She rubbed her fingers into her scalp as she walked with the kids to the van. She kept rehearsing the conference with Tyler's teacher over and over in her mind.

"Tyler seems more moody and angry lately...."
"His assignments are only half completed..."
"Is there anything going on at home I should be aware of?"

Tyler obviously needed some special attention. A bit more TLC. Where would the time come from?

She checked her watch and groaned. There was so little time before church started. "Hey, kids, how about eating out for dinner tonight?" They cheered and she smiled. That was always one sure fire way to make the kids happy.

As they climbed into the van, she eyed Tyler in the rearview mirror. "What do you think, Jen...should we let it be Tyler's pick tonight?" She was rewarded with his big, endearing grin. "McDonalds, Mom!"

McDonalds it was. As they ordered in the drive-thru, she intended to get a salad for herself, but she was still so hungry. *Ah well, one burger and order of fries never killed anybody. I'll do better tomorrow.*

The children chatted about their day as she drove. Her cell phone rang and she answered. "Hello?"

"Hey, babe. Just wanted to let you know that I got slammed at work so I'll be home late, okay?"

She sighed, trying to tamp down her resentment. "Oh, Mike. Really? Again?"

He sounded apologetic. "I'm sorry, darling. I don't like it anymore than you do. But you know they're paying me overtime. We could use the money, couldn't we? Love you, babe. See you in a while."

She checked her watch and groaned. It was too late to go home. Might as well head straight to church.

~ ~ ~

As she and the kids entered the church building, Leeanne Moore came running towards her. *Uh-oh. She looks like she wants something.*

As the kids ran off to their classes, she turned to face the out-of-breath Leeanne. "Susan! Am I glad to see you! We have a problem…"

She tried not to wince.

"Rose can't make it tonight and she usually teaches the Tiny Tots. Can you teach them, please?"

Resentment boiled up hot and strong. Rose was forever skipping out on her Wednesday night class. Sometimes she knew days before that she couldn't come but waited until the last minute to push off the class on someone else.

"Well, Leeanne, I don't know…"

"Oh please? I would take it but I'm already teaching the Beginners and the Primaries tonight." Her brown eyes turned pleading.

Susan looked longingly towards the sanctuary, where the adults were gathering for their weekly Bible study. She craved that time to soak in some Bible time. It seemed like she'd barely had time to crack open her Bible in the past several weeks. Still, it wasn't Leeanne's fault that Rose was irresponsible.

Her headache pounded sharper and exhaustion felt seeped into every pore of her body. *Susan, this is your Christian duty.*

Hiding her resentment, she smiled and heard herself saying, "Sure. I would love to…"

~ ~ ~

Nearly two hours later, she and the kids wearily dragged into the house. How could fifteen tiny tots wreak so much havoc? Jennifer and Tyler looked ready to drop. They placed their backpacks on the floor near the front door, and yawning, walked up the stairs to their rooms. Before she could blink, they would probably be passed out in their pajamas. She tried not to envy their freedom.

Biting her lip, she shot a glance at their backpacks. Both were likely full of homework assignments and notes, but she couldn't bear to make them do any work so late. *Tomorrow will be better...* It had to be.

Seems like she had been telling herself that an awful lot lately. The pain in her head had intensified to the point of being nearly unbearable. She crossed the living room and heard Mike's snores before she discovered his sleeping form on the couch. He lay stretched out on the sofa, still in his work clothes, now rumpled from sleep. Dark circles shadowed his eyes. *Poor man is worn out.* Well, who in this house wasn't?

She wondered if he had eaten at all. Guilt snaked through her. If she was a better wife, she would figure out how to at least juggle everything and fix a nice hot meal for her family. But who was she kidding? *She* couldn't even find time to eat. Worries about Tyler flittered back through her mind. She glanced at the rise and fall of Mike's chest as he dozed. Was Tyler missing his Dad? They had seen so little of each other lately.

She shuffled into the kitchen and rummaged through the cabinet for Tylenol. Finding the empty bottle, she felt overcome with exhaustion. Just one more thing she was behind on. Getting groceries.

The dirty dishes from their morning's breakfast taunted her from the table. She placed them in the sink and filled them with hot water. That would have to do for now.

She shuffled up the stairs, each step feeling like a battle. Entering her bedroom, she flopped on to the bed with a sigh of satisfaction. Finally!

Before she could sink into the bed's softness, an alarm went off in her mind. *PTO...brownies...tomorrow.* She'd forgotten to run by Walmart. Overwhelmed by all her responsibilities, the never-ending mountain she had to continually climb made her want to run away screaming into the night. *If I could just escape...*

A tear rolled down her cheek just before she heard herself praying, *Lord, this can't be the victorious life You promised...*

Hollow Victory

"A pearl is a beautiful thing that is produced by an injured life. It is the tear that forms from the injury of the oyster. The treasure of our being in this world is also produced by an injured life. If we had not been wounded, if we had not been injured, then we will not produce the pearl."
~Stephan Hoeller

Can you relate to Susan's story? For me, it struck far too familiar a chord. At least, in the scope of how my life used to be.

If you grew up in church, especially if you grew up singing hymns in the church, you've likely heard songs like "Victory in Jesus", "Faith is the Victory", "Victory Ahead" and "Victory All the Time".

But have you ever gone through a time and thought, "I don't feel victorious at all"? Maybe it was even more than that. Maybe you thought this whole victorious thing was just a great big illusion. Or maybe there was something wrong with you, because you just weren't feeling it. Everyone around you seemed to have their 'stuff' figured out. But not you. You felt like you were limping and bleeding through the Christian race.

Maybe you were even ready to quit altogether. Believe me, I understand. I've been there. If you've ever wrestled with these thoughts, or can relate to Susan in the previous story, this book is for you.

So what does it mean to have a 'hollow victory'? The idiom definition of 'hollow victory' is "where someone wins something in name, but are seen not to have gained anything by winning". Whew! Does this sound all too familiar?

In trying to come up with a good analogy for this idea, a particular childhood memory kept coming to mind.

I was at the fair with my family and had spent a fun but exhausting day of riding the scrambler and the teacups, throwing darts at balloons and walking for what seemed to be miles. I remember feeling particularly hungry. Ravenous, actually.

My parents took me to a food vendor and asked me what I wanted. I could smell the salty aroma of hot dogs and nachos...but those didn't catch my eye. All I could see was a pink, fluffy mound of cotton candy.

I pointed, "I want that!" My Mom shook her head. "That won't fill you up, honey. You'll still be hungry." But no, I had to have that glorious confection. It looked filling. After all, it was *big*. I just knew it would fill up my stomach and give me the energy I needed. Not to mention it was a pretty color. (Sounds like a girl, huh?)

After relentless pleading, my parents gave in and bought me a large bag heaped to the brim with the cottony candy. I pulled off a chunk and popped it into my mouth. The sweet treat immediately melted, leaving my mouth hollow and a sick feeling in my stomach. What had happened?

I got my way...kind of. I suppose you could say that I was victorious over what my parents wanted me to get but actually lost what I needed. A full stomach. I was beyond disappointed and cranky by the end of the night.

Have you ever fought with your spouse or loved one and thought you 'won' the argument only to discover that the issue still wasn't resolved? The underlying problem kept rearing it's ugly head. Oh, you may have won the war of words but actually never really resolved the problem.

This concept reminds me of the little boy and his grandma. The grandma is babysitting her little grandson and all day long the little boy keeps asking his grandma to croak like a frog. Struggling with a sore throat and not feeling particularly well, the grandma shakes her head and refuses. Over and over the little boy asks, driving his grandma to distraction.

Finally after hours of pleading, the little boy says, "*Please*, Grandma, croak for me!" Reaching her breaking point, the grandma sighs in exasperation and 'croaks' despite her sore throat. She gives him a sour look and asks, "Mercy sakes, why is it so important to you that I croak like a frog?"

The little boy grinned and replied, "Because Mom and Dad said that when you finally croak, we can go to Disneyland!"

Assuming A 'Win' Means To Win

You see, sometimes in our Christian walk, we assume that victory, a 'win' if you will, automatically guarantees a perfect and victorious life.

But then illness emerges. A loved one is taken away. Depression slams into us like a freight train. Suddenly, the 'win' doesn't feel like a win at all. We are left feeling hollow and abandoned. All those beautiful promises feel like an illusion.

Why? Because sometimes we assumed victory meant that we wouldn't have to deal with any underlying problems we had struggled with before. They would just naturally work out on their own. But they didn't.

And when we haven't dealt with our underlying issues, they unintentionally become underground landmines. Let's take a deeper look...

Limping Through the Victory March

If you're a believer, you know that you're in the middle of a battle, right?

"For we do not wrestle against flesh and blood, but against the rulers, against the authorities, against the cosmic powers over this present darkness, against the spiritual forces of evil in the heavenly places."
~Ephesians 6:12

That makes us soldiers in God's army. And that's exactly the idea behind those songs we grew up singing about victory. God wins, satan loses and everything is rosy.

Um, not always.

Satan is a crafty enemy. He doesn't come at us from the obvious front lines. Sometimes he traps us. He trips us up. And sometimes he even plants landmines to knock us down. And those landmines are exactly what this book is all about.

So what does a landmine do? It stays hidden, buried in rock and dirt. A field riddled with landmines looks serene and innocent from the surface. You walk along, oblivious to the disastrous danger lurking nearby. Then one step forward...and an explosion rocks your world.

I'm sure you've heard the horror stories of the victims of landmines. Severed limbs, shattered bones, blood, maimed bodies and even death. Not a pretty picture.

And here's the especially painful part: we all have these landmines buried in our lives.

Have you ever asked the question Susan did? *Lord, where is the victorious life You promised?* The reason 'victory' seems hollow and empty to you is that you might have experienced a spiritual landmine.

Sometimes the landmine is planted by the enemy; a deliberate attempt to attack as part of the spiritual warfare mentioned above. But sometimes the landmine is a struggle that you've never bothered to acknowledge before. A past abuse. A hidden secret. You may not have even been consciously aware of it. So instead of deactivating it, you let it lay dormant under the surface, refusing to acknowledge it. Until BOOM! It grabs your attention with astounding force.

Let's look at this from another angle...

Hollow Victory · 30

LANDMINES: WHERE DO THEY COME FROM, ANYWAY?

The Big Hole Inside

Ever since we as humans messed up in the Garden of Eden, we have a hole inside. That connection with God was severed when we sinned. He is purity and purity cannot co-exist with filth. Otherwise, it ceases to be pure.

So we try to fill that hole with something: approval, drugs, alcohol, sex, relationships, attention, pride, food...the list is endless. But none of those things ever really satisfy us, do they?

In his book *Searching for God Knows What,* Donald Miller explains this in great detail.

> *"It makes you feel that as a parent the most important thing you can do is love your kids, hold them and tell them you love them because, until we get to heaven, all we can do is hold our palms over the wounds. I mean, if a kid doesn't feel he is loved, he is going to go looking for it in all kinds of ways. He is going to want to feel powerful or important or tough, and she is going to want to feel*

beautiful and wanted and needed. Give a kid the feeling of being loved early, and they will be better at negotiating that other stuff when they get older. They won't fall for anything stupid, and they won't feel a kind of desperation all the time in their souls."

He continues:

"It feels like we all have these little acts, these stupid things we do that we all hang our hats on. The Fall has made monkeys of us, for crying out loud. Some of us are athletes and others of us are physicists, and some of us are good-looking and some of us are rich, and we all are running around, in a way, trying to get a bunch of people to clap for us, trying to get a bunch of people to say we are normal, we are healthy, we are good. And there is nothing wrong with being beautiful or being athletic or being smart, but those are some of the pleasures of life, not life's redemption."

Finding the Wound

So what happens when something is severed? Yep, it's separated. It leaves a mess behind. A bloody, gaping wound.

Hollow Victory will look at five different landmines that can lead you to a broken and battered Christian life and we'll explore just how they got there in the first place. These landmines are grief, depression, people-pleasing, perfectionism, and fear (anxiety). There are many more landmines not discussed in this book, but these are good places to start. And consequently, ones I have struggled with intimately. These problems seemingly lie dormant for years and then explode in breath-taking ways, leaving its victim bleeding and in pain.

Each of us has one of those wounds inside. We try to pack the hole with all kinds of stuff to soothe it. We try to bandage it over and over again, or even ignore it but unless we expose it (and deactivate it) it will never heal.

But how can you discover what your wound is? Let me blow your mind for a minute here. Your wound is NOT one of issues we will discuss in this book. It's not depression, people-pleasing, perfectionism, grief or fear. These problems are just symptoms of the wound. You can discover what your wound is by what you try to use to fill it.

Does it still feel murky? Okay, I'll give you an example. You're going to hear all about my battle with depression. My particular depression issue was a result of exhaustion. Why was I exhausted? Because I was running around like a lunatic trying to keep everybody happy. Pleasing people was my bread and butter.

But people-pleasing is not my wound. It's a little deeper than that. Why do I need approval so much? I seem to equate approval with love. So I was trying to feel loved. My wound is that I feel unloved.

I know this can be a bit scary. But don't flinch. Don't run away from it. I would say to do just the opposite it. **Embrace it**. This is the only way to find freedom and healing...and ultimately, real victory in your life.

Taking a Look Inside

Do you battle depression or anxiety? Are you exhausted from trying to please everyone around you? Have you dealt with a string of broken relationships? Are you wrapped in grief from circumstances beyond your control? Are you consumed with guilt or shame? Are you craving something you can't quite define? Do you feel unloved? Do you know something is wrong inside but you just can't figure out what it is?

These are heavy questions. And the answer doesn't always lie on the surface. If 'victorious' seems a far off dream to you, you might need to confront some painful things in your life.

But I Don't Wanna!

I know, I know. It's painful. But I think so many of our 'issues', our wounds, cause us so much trouble because we refuse to confront them. We just try to cope as best we can and kind of turn on a numb form of spiritual and emotional autopilot. But soon those buried wounds comes to a head when *they* confront us. Here is what I mean...

I was hanging out in Branson, Missouri with my husband and two good friends, Tim and Amy. We had decided to drive up and enjoy some couples time for the weekend, without the stress of kids, family or work obligations. So like any group of mature, self-respecting young adults, we decided to play bumper cars.

I must stop right here and tell you that all four of us are incredibly competitive. Bumper cars is not just a game to us...it's cut-throat! It's also inexpensive. We decided to spend all day whacking the stuffing out of each other. After six hours of non-stop flashing lane lights, bone-breaking jolts, friendly revenge and smelling corn dogs from the food court, my brain was on overload. We played so long that I knew I could drive one of those killer cars in my sleep.

Late that afternoon we decided we'd tortured the employees of the bumper car business long enough. We dragged our sore, tired muscles back into our Grand Am car. All four of us were tired but smiling as we recounted the day's slaughter. My husband pulled out into traffic on highway 76. When he spotted a blue Chevy about an eighth of a mile ahead of us, he began to accelerate. He mashed the pedal to the floor and came screaming up behind the little Chevy before my brain kicked into gear. I screamed, "STOP!!!!" as I prepared to feel the sensation of crunching metal and glass. Todd realized what was about to ensue, and he slammed the brakes with all of his might. We swerved off the road and into the side median.

All four of us looked at each other with wide, frightened eyes. That's when my brain finally registered what had just happened. We had played bumper cars for so long, that accelerating towards traffic had become habit! None of us had even realized the difference until it was almost too late.

You see, we spent so much time in our bumper car routine (accelerating, smashing, spinning and slamming) that it quickly became second nature to us. I suppose our bodies were so used to the abuse that pain, or awareness of our surroundings, didn't even register anymore.

Perty package, Perty Bow

Isn't it funny how much our Christian culture enjoys the illusion of 'perfect endings'? In trying to help each other, we try to summarize the hurting person's problem, give a solution and wrap it up with a little bow.

But life isn't like that. People are messy. And that's okay. God knows we are messy or He wouldn't have sent His Son.

One day, Jesus stood up in the middle of a crowded, Judean temple and offered the greatest invitation known to man: "If anyone is thirsty, let him come to me and drink. Whoever believes in me, as the Scripture has said, streams of living water will flow from within him." (John 7:37-38) Notice that Jesus didn't say, "How dare you be thirsty! Why don't you have you act together?"

He knows that we have a hole inside that gnaws our spirit. He knows our victory sometimes feels hollow and unfulfilling. So instead of berating our broken condition, He pleads, "Come to Me...." There is no commandment to clean ourselves up first, just a welcome invitation to be transformed. But notice that we have to take the first step.

Why Confront Our Issues?

"There is a direct correlation between your willingness to face the darkness of your own pain and your ability to live freely and fully." ~ Steve Brown

My husband's great-grandma (affectionately called 'Mimi') was a precious lady, and apparently became a handful as she got older. One morning the entire family was gathered around the table as they happily prepared to share some of her famous cake.

A family member placed a forkful in his mouth and noticed a twangy taste in the confection. Nothing specifically wrong; it was delicious as always but it had a funny flavor. After the family began chowing down and ooooohing and aaaaahhhing over her work, Mimi hollered to her husband, "See! That spoiled milk I put in that cake didn't hurt it at all!"

When we fail to root out the source of our issues, the unconfronted 'stuff' will affect every other area of our lives. It's like sour milk in a cake. It was still a cake, still pretty good but not nearly as good as it could be. What a difference fresh milk would have made!

In Larry Crabb's book *Inside Out*, the author made a brilliant point on the necessity of confronting our tough stuff.

> "The majority of people...are building their houses on sand by preserving their happiness through pretense; or, to change the image, maybe they're rearranging the furniture in the motel room, hoping it will feel like home. When we succeed at arranging our life so 'all is well', we keep ourselves from facing all that's going on inside. And when we ignore what's happening on the inside, we lose all power to change what we do on the outside in any meaningful way. We *rearrange* rather than *change*, and in so doing, we never become the transformed person God calls us to be. We never experience freedom from destructive patterns of living....Change as our Lord describes it involves more than cleaning up our visible act. He intends us to do more than sweep the streets; He wants us to climb down into the sewers and do something about the filth beneath the concrete." (*Inside Out*, p.35-6)

Did you know that Jesus' harshest words of criticism were reserved for the religious folks who "had it together"? If we take a look in the gospels, we see that the Pharisees took denial to a whole new level.

These guys were the esteemed religious leaders of the Jews. And they specialized in looking good. They were completely performance driven. They longed for the respect of the masses. Pharisees were the 'we have it together' clique. And most folks put them on a pedestal because of it.

But you know, what I love about Jesus is His ability to cut past the pretty package and strip away all the fluff to find what's inside. He wasn't fooled by their trimmings, their power or prestige. He saw their hearts...and consequently, their issues. In Matthew 23, this is what He had to say to them:

> *"Woe to you, teachers of the law and Pharisees, you hypocrites! You give a tenth of your spices — mint, dill and cummin. But you have neglected the more important matters of the law---justice, mercy and faithfulness. You should have practiced the latter, without neglecting the former...You clean the outside of the cup and dish, but inside they are full of greed and self-indulgence. Blind Pharisee! First clean the inside of the cup and dish, and then the outside will also be clean. You are like whitewashed tombs, which look beautiful on the outside but on the inside are full of dead men's bones and everything unclean. In the same way, on the outside you appear to people as righteous but on the inside you are full of hypocrisy and wickedness." (verses 23-28 NIV)*

Ouch! Tough words but honest. Jesus was desperately, and as bluntly as possible, trying to make them take a look inside. Change cannot come without it. But the Pharisees were furious. They couldn't handle the hurt and pain. Denial was an easier route.

His words still challenge us today. To have the best and happiest life possible, denial and pretense should have no part in your life. He wants each of us to be courageous enough to come to grips with the issues we fight behind our whitewashed walls.

Although it's uncomfortable, struggling through this tough stuff gives life. Consider the words of Ray Comfort:

"A man once watched a butterfly struggling to get out of its cocoon. In an effort to help it, he took a razor blade and carefully slit the edge of the cocoon. The butterfly escaped from its problem----and immediately died. It is God's way to have the butterfly struggle. It is the struggle that causes its tiny heart to beat fast and to send the life's blood into its wings. Trials have their purpose. They make us struggle----they bring us to our knees. They are the cocoon in which we often find ourselves."

Turning on the Light Bulb

Awareness is half the battle, in my opinion. As you'll discover later, I learned some very tough lessons the hard way, simply because I walked around in a numb fog, oblivious to my own wounds until the danger exploded, knocking me down.

In other words, you can't heal what isn't exposed.

If you have continuing problems with depression, anxiety, broken relationships, or sadness (to name a few), a deeper look inside might be needed. Life is too short to live burdened and unhappy. Today is a gift...don't ignore it by refusing to accept it! For the victorious life to feel like a lie was never, ever God's intention!

In my yard I have some gorgeous hibiscus plants. I'm not exaggerating when I say that some of the crimson blossoms are larger than the span of my hand. Each year I look forward to watching them bloom again; beautiful to the eye and a scent that is heavenly.

I quickly learned though that unless I was willing to cut back those branches each fall, the hibiscus would suffer greatly when spring rolled around. They would look thin, scraggly and unhealthy. So although I hate snipping those lovely plants back, they will be much healthier down the road. Not just healthy, but thriving and gorgeous.

This might be your own 'pruning' time.

Are you Ready for a Shake Up?

"Sores represent hurt but scars represent healing. The scars of your past are a clear indication that you've been healed delivered and set free!"
~ Marshall Newsome

What is the similarity between Calvary, Jericho and Paul and Silas' time in prison? In each instance, the place was shaken because God showed up. And He wants to do the same with you.

A shake up can be scary, but it's also exciting and it reminds us of God's power. (Not to mention it's life-changing impact.) It's time to face your wounds, embrace them, understand them and see what God does. I promise you, when He turns up, it's going to be BIG! Those same landmines that have the potential to hurt you can also make you turn to Him for healing, *if* you let them knock you down to your knees.

So let's stop for a minute and think, how can you render a landmine powerless? You can step on it, as we often do, but it damages us in the process. How do we make it ineffective?

We have to disarm it.

Sometimes part of the 'shake up' is intentionally exploding those landmines. Being purposeful in disarming them is a huge key to being free from their danger.

During this past year, I realized that I've prayed for lots of things in my walk with Christ, but I have never, ever prayed for boldness. Maybe because it's a scary process, much like praying for patience. I mentally cringed, thinking *Lord, I want to be brave...fearless. Give me boldness. But not too fast. Be gentle!*

If you're ready, we're going to take gentle steps forward and look at the landmines lurking in our lives. My friend Sherrie said it this way, "It's true that God parted the Red Sea for His children; but they had to be willing to walk through. It takes His power *and* our willingness." Are you ready to take a look inside, discover some common landmines and figure out how to disarm them?

Landmine #1: Grief

"This too shall pass...maybe like a kidney stone, but it WILL pass."
~My Mom

Grief is one of those landmines that everybody will experience at some time or another. Some losses are expected and they hurt, but then there are those that seem like a cruel joke, squeezing the breath out us, leaving us devastated and unable to move. The problem with this landmine is that it leaves you feeling abandoned on the battle field.

Where is God?

Where is God? I hear this question often. It's easy to praise Him when things are going great. It's easy to sense Him with you when everything in your world is at peace.

But what about when the unthinkable occurs? The loss of a child or spouse. The terrifying trip to the ER. The cancer diagnosis that has just rocked your world. When I miscarried my babies, everything I knew about God was yanked out from under me, leaving me teetering in shock. Pain squeezed my heart in a vice grip that made it hard to draw a breath. All I could ask is "Why?" Of course, no thundering voice interrupted my pleas. No wind blew. Where was He?

In his book *Where is God?*, John Townsend states, *"We are not a people who perceive reality as it truly is 100 percent of the time.*

Our internal 'lens' fogs up and distorts what is going on...to be perfectly honest, we often don't care what the lesson or purpose is behind the scenes...most of the time we just want the trouble to end so we can go back to life."

This is true, isn't it? The friend who says "This terrible experience is going to grow you" runs the risk of a smack across the face.

People tend to like security. We want to know the game plan. It's like preparing for surgery: the surgeon explains exactly what's going to happen and gives the patient an opportunity to grill him about anything they are uncertain of. He explains the procedure, how long it will take to heal, the possible complications, how it will help and each step that will be part of the process. This puts the patient's mind at ease. Does this mean that everything will go perfectly? No, but the patient *feels* better because they are mentally and emotionally prepared. They feel like they have a sense of control over the situation.

What's Going On?

I have two little dogs named Elvis and Sugar. When I come home they are beyond excited. Running, jumping, squealing...party time! But when I have to leave, they look at me sadly with their big, brown puppy eyes filled with anxiety and confusion. They don't understand what's going on. Why I'm leaving or when I'll be back.

Now, I know that I'm only running to Walmart for thirty minutes, but they don't. That sort of understanding is beyond them. All they know is that I am leaving and they will be left alone.

It's a similar relationship between us and God. We don't really have the capacity to understand all the ins and outs of 'why'...but He does.

"As the heavens are higher than the earth, so are my ways higher than your ways and my thoughts than your thoughts."
~Isaiah 55:9

Daddy, There's A Monster Under My Bed!

What does a child do when they are in danger, whether real or perceived? They usually run to one of their parents. "Daddy, there's a monster under my bed!" And what does the parent do? Comforts, consoles, absorbs their child's emotions until they feel calm once again.

If we have been redeemed, God is our Father. "For you have not received the spirit of bondage again to fear; but you have received the Spirit of adoption, whereby we cry, Abba, Father." (Romans 8:15) "Abba" can be translated as "Daddy". Isn't that beautiful? God is our Daddy. So when tragedy strikes, it's normal to run for our Daddy's arms. To let him reassure us, comfort us, and fight those monsters away. But sometimes it seems like we run and can't find Him. And our fear increases.

But you know what? Just because we didn't expect that tragedy to come, doesn't mean that God has suddenly disappeared. And He never promised we wouldn't deal with some tough stuff. This world is not how He designed it. Ever since the sin curse, we are broken and messy people. But He did promise that He would hold us as we go through our disaster and give us His strength to survive.

Free will comes with a high price. And God gave us that very thing: free will. We are free to follow Him, to walk with Him, to let Him love us. Or as a human race, we are also free to follow our own desires. And that's where we mess up. I would daresay that the majority of sorrows and problems we face in this life are a result of the consequences of other people's bad choices, not because there is an angry God trying to make us miserable.

I have seen it happen over and over again. I've had multiple friends who, after facing a crisis that shattered their world, would shake their fist at the sky, vowing never to trust God again. But God loves them too much to give up. Just like a patient Mom or Dad, He takes his tantrum-throwing child into His arms and rocks them until they calm down. He gently whispers into their ear until their screams of anger turn to gentle sobbing. He holds them tightly until those sobs relax into cleansing breaths. And at that moment, acceptance comes. And sometimes, even an understanding of why it happened in the first place.

And yes, you will have those moments when you'll have to operate on what you *know*...not how you *feel*. That is faith. And it's trusting that our Father knows why.

So let's dig deeper and focus on landmine number one: dealing with grief. I'll start by sharing my own story....

Grief Section 2: December's Songbird

Have you ever heard someone ask, "Why do bad things happen to good people?" or the ever popular "Well, if God is so good, why am I suffering?" Both good questions, both have stumped theologians the world over, but both have an answer.

My pastor says that there are three certainties in life: you are either in the middle of a storm, you're coming out of a storm, or you're about to enter a storm. In the fall of 2009, my little family entered a time of extreme financial distress. We had a rent house that was destroyed by a renter who owed thousands in back payments and found ourselves unable to find a buyer. My husband's health began to crash due to stress and I had to take on two extra jobs to make ends meet. Logically speaking, each month we should have run out of money. But each month the money was there in our account. I know it was a God thing. He takes care of His kids.

It seemed like whatever we touched during this time would crash and burn. I began to look for the biblical plague of locust on the horizon. Until I got the news: I was expecting again.

We were overjoyed and thought maybe the tide was beginning to turn. Maybe God was moving us into a better place. Maybe....just maybe.

My kids were thrilled and I spent my days daydreaming about whether the baby was a boy or a girl, picking names, telling our family. That little baby became our symbol of God's goodness, of hope.

Several weeks before Christmas, I began to hemorrhage. My husband rushed me to the hospital and after a night in the ER and several tests, the doctor came to see me, shaking her head and telling me she was sorry but the baby was gone. It seemed like a dream. I could hear the doctor talking but couldn't focus on what she was saying. There was a buzzing in my ears. I felt salt in my mouth and realized with a start I was crying. I walked out of that ER feeling abandoned, broken and numb.

I would love to say that I cried myself to sleep that night, but sleep never came. I cried all night, alternating between disbelief and pain as the reality of our loss fell fresh in my heart again. I lay facing our large window, watching as the first streaks of sun painted the night sky. And that's when I heard it.

A lone, solitary bird singing its heart out.

Just speaking for the state of Arkansas, birds don't chirp in the dead of winter. It's too cold, too miserable. Yet I heard it just the same.

I rose from my bed and walked slowly to my window, looking out at our pond and meadow, trying to find the source of that sweet music. My breath fogged the cold glass. As I stood there empty and vulnerable, I realized with a start that the little bird I heard was making a choice: despite the cold, despite what the rest of nature was doing, that little bird chose to rise from his bed and sing.

So I faced a choice: I could either rail against my Maker, blame God and let the bitterness consume me, or I could praise Him. Praise Him for the weeks that He gave me rejoicing and nurturing His creation. Praise Him that He sees the big picture and really does know what's best. Rejoice that because of Jesus, I would see my child again. I raised my face to the sky and whispered the words of Job, "The Lord has given and the Lord has taken away. Blessed be the name of the Lord!"

Several months later, I rejoiced to discover I was expecting yet again. I thought we had weathered the storm, came out victorious, and God was getting ready to pour out more blessings. I was wrong---the storm continued. At almost four months along, I miscarried again.

It would be a lie for me to say that I sensed God's presence with me during the second miscarriage. I didn't. I felt abandoned, alone and broken. I kept praying *Father God, is there some secret sin that I've been harboring that I'm not even aware of? Why? Why is this happening again?* Then I got mad. Not mad at God, but mad at Adam, at Eve and that awful, lying snake!

God never promised that we wouldn't have heartache. He never promised that we would never face cancer. He never promised that we wouldn't suffer the horror of abuse. But what He did promise was that no matter what life throws our way, He would walk us through it. *"And lo, I am with you always, even unto the end of the age."* He is with us in the ICU. He is with us in our empty houses. He is with us when everything crashes down. He is there.

Around the same time I miscarried for the second time, a friend of mine lost her baby too. She turned to me one day and asked, "Tara, are we cursed?" I thought for a moment and replied, "Yep. It's called the sin curse!" I have had to remind myself that the sin curse is not God's fault. It's ours. Thanks to Adam, Eve and our enemy (who, I confess I am still pretty mad at) we live in a world full of disease and broken people. It is a mess we have created and one that we will have to deal with until Jesus returns.

The morning that I lost my first baby, when I heard that little bird's frigid whistle and chose to praise God for the child I lost, I lay back down in my bed and tucked my knees up to my chest. I just listened to the song. So similar to Christ's song: a song that gave glory to God despite the agony. As I lay there, peace seemed to cover me like a blanket. I felt like the Lord had cuddled right up beside me, much a like a father or mother embraces a hurting child. I sensed His arms around me and felt love unlike any other time in my life. He didn't abandon me; indeed, He was there.

Every time I hear a bird's gentle whistle, I'm reminded of December's songbird...and I smile. I know that praise isn't just designed for the moments when life is joyous. Praise is a choice.

GRIEF SECTION 3: BUT DON'T TAKE MY WORD FOR IT...

I can only speak for myself; out of my experience and what God has shown me. So I thought you might like to read the experiences of several of my friends, and what God revealed to them during their darkest hours.

An Interview with Debra

Debra and I met back in 2011 at the American Christian Fiction Writers Conference in St. Louis, Missouri. We both share a love of good fiction, writing, and all things southern. (Who says people from Alabama and Arkansas can't get along?) We hit it off immediately but little did I know the pain my friend had experienced....

Have you ever struggled with depression or grief?

Only during the time that I lost my daughter. It was more grief than depression. You learn so much going through something like that. Tosha was getting ready to get married. *(Quiet for a moment)* You never expect to wake up and have to plan your child's funeral.

What were the days like for you after she passed?

After Tosha died, I asked God every night to take my life, even with my other three kids still living. I've always loved singing in church. But I stopped singing. I was like a zombie...I was so, so angry with God.

(*Reflective for a few moments*) I'll never forget Christmas that year. I found a knot in my throat. (*Begins to cry*) I prayed that it was cancer. I wanted to die so badly.

What happened?

(*Smiles*) I was at the hospital and was walking out of the building. I was filled with so much anger. I remember telling God "I'll never praise You again. You took my child."

I was wrapped up in my own grief but as I was leaving, I saw a lady in the parking lot that attended my church. She was sobbing. So I walked up to her and asked her if she was okay. Through her tears, she shared that her dad had just passed.

God poured out His love and compassion in me in that parking lot. I remember wrapping my arms around her, murmuring words of comfort. I reminded her of God's promises and His love. (*laughs*) I had just told Him moments before that I would never praise Him again and here I was sharing His love and comfort with another hurting soul. Out of my own need, I prayed for her needs.

In that moment, He healed me. Emotionally, mentally and physically. And after that day I never questioned Him again. I remember praying, "God, You are God. You know. You don't have to answer my questions anymore."

The next week, I returned to the doctor's office to find out whether the lump in my throat was cancerous or not. The doctor was baffled to discover the knot was gone.

Wow!

From that day on, God started doing a work with me; helping others who have lost children.

What would you tell people to do to help their heart-broken friend?

Oh goodness, there's so much yet there's also nothing a person can do. For me, there was nothing that anyone could say that made it better. Only God can do that.

Through my own grieving process, I learned what NOT to say.

(laughs) Yes! People will unintentionally hurt your feelings. Now I just say, when comforting others, "I love you. I'm here for you anytime."

A pastor told me, "I know what you're going through because my mother passed away a few months ago." I got angry. I thought "No! You don't know. You lost your mother but you have no idea what it's like to lose a child!"

One lady at the funeral home told me "I know what you're going through. And you'll NEVER get over it." I thought "Then why should I even try to have a life?" Bless her heart, she was trying to empathize but she only made me feel even more like my life was over. It's always better to just say, "I love you", drop a meal by the house...things like that.

I want to live one day at a time. We never know when it's our last day, and we never know when it's someone else's last day. But I don't believe in looking back with regret. Anymore, I just live each day like it's my last day.

~ ~ ~

An Interview with Linda

One afternoon, I stood in the book section of the Mardel store in Little Rock, gazing indecisively at the number of novels I wanted to purchase. It's hard to buy ten books when you only have $15 in your pocket!

Sighing, I turned and look down the aisle, only to see my good friend R.C. chatting with a pretty lady. A few moments later, he introduced me to the great Linda Miller. And yes, I say great because she is easily one of the most gifted poets I've ever known. We ended up chatting for close to an hour that day and I found a kindred spirit.

Linda is kind, creative, gentle and a huge supporter of my music ministry. After hearing her story, I asked if I could interview her for this book project. And of course, she obliged.

Your poetry is such a blessing. They always lift me up.

I'm getting better about being honest. *(laughs)* No matter what, I've discovered a person can always be a good example…or a bad one! So ultimately no matter what you share, you'll never be a failure. No one is perfect.

Recently I've decided to be more open and honest. I've cracked the window of my own little world. I try not to worry about whether I'll be judged. I've just been focusing on talking to people and getting to know them as a person. I have to brave enough to not worry about what others think of me when I share.

Well, I always love talking with you…you have amazing insight!

(laughs) My insight is just called mileage.

You know, it is something that is natural for me, I guess. Sharing what is so personal. My granddad committed suicide when my father was young. The family saw it. So although my father was incredibly loving and kind, he didn't talk about anything personal or painful. My baby brother died not long after being born and nobody talked about it. Not my Dad. Not even my Mom. I don't even know where he is buried because no one ever spoke of him again.

But in searching for answers about stuff like that, I have learned a lot about myself. Helping other people sometimes pushes my own stuff to the back burner, but in helping them, God also ministers to me. He heals me as I help others through their painful stuff.

Isn't it crazy and wonderful how He works like that?

At five a.m., I woke up with a thought this morning. You know, many people have trouble seeing things in black and white. But God does! I was mulling this over in my mind and I thought, "What you see is determined by the color of glasses you put on."

Oooo, I like that!

Some people put on rose-colored glasses; everything looks perfect. Some wear green; they are full of envy. A depressed person might look through shades of blue or something dark, like sunglasses. And of course, for those with bad eyesight, you just see through the glass darkly! *(laughs)*

Did you ever have a moment in your life when you thought "This isn't how I thought life was going to be?"

(long pause) Yes. My grandparents passed away before I had my own children. I always mourned that my children would never know, or be held be them. I remember standing outside one day, by myself, hands raised to God and praying, "Thank you, anyways, Father. You are so good!" My husband and I determined that we would do all we could to attend every family function reunion, etc. so our kids could have those family memories.

Then we began losing one person a year. And these were the family members that were very close to us. By the time I was 27, we had lost the majority of our family. It was me, my husband, our two young kids and two widows to take care of who had fourteen children between the two of them. That's the time when I thought "Uh, this isn't what I thought it would be."

I just so desperately wanted to 'turn the page'…get past it all. Then a year later, my husband Jack died.

Goodness…so much tragedy.

Life is usually what happens when you are making other plans. *(long pause)* Some bad stuff comes from choices and some from circumstances. But what matters are your responses to both.

~ ~ ~

When God is Silent

I think the key to overcoming grief is in Linda's last statement: *"What matters are your responses to both."* The unexpected, the consequences of others…when tough times come, sometimes it seems relentless! We can't control what happens in this life, but we can control our response.

The hardest part, though, is when you desperately long for God's touch, His presence, but you can't find Him. That feeling of being shattered on the battlefield and abandoned to boot.

When I lost my babies Taylor and Morgan, the pain squeezing around my heart made it hard to breathe. And no matter where I turned, the devastation confronted me; refusing to let me rest, refusing to let me forget.

But as I quieted the questions plaguing my heart, Jesus began to whisper to me. "I'm here. You are my princess. I love you. I love those sweet babies. I'm looking at them right now...and they're happy. Just rest. Let me hold you for awhile..."

There is a blessed peace that comes with surrender. With learning that it's okay not to have the answers. Just because God is silent doesn't mean that He's disappeared. He is there...waiting. Waiting for you to crawl up in His lap and let Him love on you.

As anyone who has gone through a tragedy knows, sometimes words make it worse. Well meaning phrases meant to comfort only bring hollow promises and more pain. It's simply not enough to say 'it will be okay' when everything going on around you tells you it won't be okay anymore. Not this time.

The best comfort I received were from friends who gave me a hug and said "I love you". No platitudes. No resounding words of wisdom. Just love.

In some ways, I think this is what God does. He doesn't fill our spirits with empty, meaningless clichés. He lets us cry, lets us mourn and wraps His arms around us when it gets to be too much.

> *"The LORD said, 'Go out and stand on the mountain in the presence of the LORD, for the LORD is about to pass by.' Then a great and powerful wind tore the mountains apart and shattered the rock before the LORD, but the LORD was not in the wind. After the wind there was an earthquake, but the LORD was not in the earthquake. After the earthquake came a fire, but the LORD was not in the fire. And after the fire came a gentle whisper."*
>
> *~ I Kings 19:11-12*

Sometimes, when God is silent, it's simply because He's listening.

Hollow Victory · 56

GRIEF SECTION 4: DEVELOPING A 20/20 PERSPECTIVE

"I can no more understand the totality of God than the pancake I made for breakfast understands the complexity of me."

~ Donald Miller *Blue like Jazz*

We are creatures with a very small window.

Our view, our perception and our vision is limited. Extremely so. And because of that, when a tragedy strikes it seems *big* to us. And it is.

We cannot dismiss our feelings but it often helps to take a step back and remember God from a historical perspective; and to take a deep breath and try to look at things from the 'big picture' viewpoint.

"This ability is one of the traits of maturity. Children don't come packaged with it. For them, the present it all that matters. There is no other reality that they care about. Our kids have never said 'Thanks for the broccoli. I know it doesn't taste as good as pizza, but the nutrients are more wholesome.'...That ability to see other factors comes with time and has to be developed. This is simply true for us in life, in love, in career, and in understanding hard times." (John Townsend, *Where is God?*)

Very few people have developed this ability as deeply as Betsy and Corrie Ten Boom. Sentenced to a Nazi extermination camp after working to lead many Dutch Jews to freedom, these two sisters had the innate ability to focus on the big picture and see the handiwork of God, despite their pain. As Corrie herself said, "When a train goes through a tunnel and it gets dark, you don't throw away the ticket and jump off. You sit still and trust the engineer."

Corrie's poem *Life is but a Weaving* explains this perspective incredibly well:

> My life is but a weaving
> Between my God and me.
> I cannot choose the colors
> He weaveth steadily.
> Oft' times He weaveth sorrow;
> And I in foolish pride
> Forget He sees the upper
> And I the underside.
> Not 'til the loom is silent
> And the shuttles cease to fly
> Will God unroll the canvas
> And reveal the reason why.
> The dark threads are as needful
> In the weaver's skillful hand
> As the threads of gold and silver
> In the pattern He has planned
> He knows, He loves, He cares;
> Nothing this truth can dim.
> He gives the very best to those
> Who leave the choice to Him.

Taking A Lesson From History

When I am really feeling bummed out, it helps to be able to look back at the great heroes of faith from the Bible: Job, David, Ruth...these are people who went though some terribly hard losses but were able to cling to their faith in

God. And because of their story, we have 20/20 hindsight glimpse into God's master plan for their lives.

And if He blessed them beyond the tragedies, He can bless you too. It's important to observe how they responded to grief; it's instructive to us.

It's also important to note that loss doesn't always mean the loss of a person. It could be the loss of a job. The loss of health. The loss of reputation. You feel what you feel. There are no right or wrongs with emotions. The Bible affirms the need to grieve and express sorrow. But the question is, how will you respond in times of grief?

Job

Was there ever another human who endured so much tragedy? In one single, horrible day, Job lost his wealth, his home, his health, the respect of his wife and all of his children in one chilling swoop. Talk about a landmine! *(Read all of Job chapter 1 and answer the questions in the Study Guide on page 5 for an even deeper understanding.)*

I can't even fathom such grief! It reads like a bad soap opera, doesn't it? Yet notice Job's response. Upon hearing of all the devastation, Job tore his robe and shaved his head (a sign of intense mourning in the middle east), but then fell to the ground in worship and said, 'The LORD has given and the LORD has taken away; blessed be the name of the LORD.' (Job 1:20-21) He grieved and he praised.

Grieving is not wrong. Indeed, it's actually a healthy response to suffering and loss. The friend who says, 'It's time to get over it..." has never been hit with a tragedy. But instead of blaming God, Job recognized that God was in control and the Giver of life. It's easy to praise God when things are rosy; but it takes your faith to a whole new level when you can praise Him in the midst of your catastrophes.

Job's response was essentially stating, "I don't understand. This hurts badly. But You are bigger than I am. You can see all things. And I choose to trust You even when my heart is torn in two." This takes an unheard of trust in an unseen God.

To add insult to injury, Job's friends come by and visit him in the midst of his misery. Instead of comforting him, they only bring him more pain with their questions and assumptions. His own wife told him to curse God and die. Job replied, " 'You are talking like a foolish woman. Shall we accept good from God, and not trouble?' In all this, Job did not sing in what he said." (Job 2:10)

Job had no idea if his trust in God would bring Him future blessings or if he would continue to be wrapped in disease and pain. But because of the written Word, we know that God rewarded him greatly because of his trust and faithfulness. *"The LORD blessed the latter part of Job's life more than the first. He had fourteen thousand sheep, six thousand camels, a thousand yokes of oxen and a thousand donkeys. And he also had seven sons and three daughters...nowhere in all the land were there found women as beautiful as Job's daughters."* (Job 42:12-15) What a beautiful reward!

An Additional Thought

Lately, I've run across several friends who are going through some tough stuff. And over and over again I hear the same murmurs of frustration... "I just don't understand God sometimes."

Join the club! If any of us could completely understand God, we would *be* God. And we're not. His ways are higher than our ways, and His thoughts than our thoughts.

But have you ever stopped to consider God's viewpoint in the book of Job? In chapter one, satan comes into the presence of God with his usual boasts and taunts. Notice God's question in verses 8. "Have you considered my servant Job? There is no one on earth like him; he is blameless and upright, a man who fears God and shuns evil." Satan goes on to reply that [paraphrased] "Of course Job loves you! You've put your hedge of protection around him! But if you remove it, I'm guessing that Job will curse you to your face."

And we know what happened: Job was put through the most agonizing test known to man. The list is dizzying. Yet after standing faithful to God, the Lord blessed the end of his life more than entirety of the beginning.

I love the way Beth Moore eloquently expounded upon this idea. *"The Lord boasting in any mortal is almost unthinkable. We feel like our feet of clay mainly just leave muddy footprints. Consider the even wilder part; God can't lie (Numbers 23:19), so His boasts are always based on truth. He permits and sometimes even dictates difficulty for those in whom He boasts so that they will prove what He already knows is truth. The Lord does not put us to tests that He knows in advance we don't have the wherewithal to pass. He boasts in His faithful followers then lets them prove Him right. Sometimes the person most shocked by the proof is the human put to the test...We always feel more romantic about suffering when we're not doing it. Still, the thought that God might boast in us puts a iron shot in our anemic souls, doesn't it? The irony may be that no greater compliment exists in this temporal realm than for God to say, 'Have you seen my servant _____?'"*

Are you brave enough to put your own name in the blank?

David

David knew the pain of losing a child. One as an infant, one murdered and another grown son who rebelled against him.

Not all grief is a result of sin in our life, but the choices we make *can* cause grief. David committed adultery with Bathsheba and then had her husband killed. Through the prophet Nathan, God told David that he would endure personal tragedies in his family because of his disobedience.

2 Samuel 12:15-23 reads:

"After Nathan had gone home, the LORD struck the child that Uriah's wife had borne to David, and he became ill. David pleaded with God for the child. He fasted and went into his house and spent the nights lying on the ground. The elders of his household stood beside him to get him up from the ground, but he refused, and he would not eat any food with them.

On the seventh day the child died. David's servants were afraid to tell him that the child was dead, for they thought 'While the child was still living, we spoke to David but he would not listen to us. How can we tell him the child is dead? He may do something desperate.' David noticed that his servants were whispering among themselves and he realized the child was dead. 'Is the child dead?' he asked. 'Yes,' they replied, 'he is dead.'

Then David got up from the ground. After he had washed, put on lotions and changed his clothes, he went into the house of the LORD and worshiped. Then he went to his own house, and at his request they served him food, and he ate.

His servants asked him, 'Why are you acting this way? While the child was alive, you fasted and wept, but now that the child is dead, you get up and eat!' He answered, 'While the child was alive, I fasted and wept. I thought, who knows? The LORD may be gracious to me and let the child live. But now that he is dead, why should I fast? Can I bring him back again? I will go to him, but he will not return to me.'"

Though this tragedy was a result of his own disobedience, David recognized vital truths about his Savior. *He knew that God was listening to him.* He sought God's mercy and even though His answer was 'no', David went to worship his Savior before He ate a bite. He also knew where his son was: in the presence of God. He knew he would see his son again.

Later, David's grown son Absalom rebelled against him, declared himself king and formed an army to overtake his father. Talk about rebelling against your Dad! The nation's loyalties were divided. In the midst of battle, David received word that Absalom had been killed.

2 Samuel 18: 33 says:

"The king was shaken. He went up to the room over the gateway and wept. As he went, he said: 'Oh my son Absalom! My son, my son Absalom! If only I had died instead of you--O Absalom, my son, my son!'"

Heartbreaking and tragic! The Scriptures tell us David mourned intensely for his son. God understands that even though we may have buried a loved one, we cannot bury our feelings. We need time to vent—and to find ways of coping with the loss in our lives. The great people of faith did not rush through the process of grief.
Neither should you.

Ruth

I admit that Ruth is one of my favorites. Her loyalty and strength are like a beacon of light in an otherwise gloomy start to her story. And it wasn't just Ruth who grieved, but her sister-in-law and mother-in-law as well.

> *"The book of Ruth tells us that Naomi was happily married to a man named Elimilech and together they had two strong sons, Mahlon and Kilion. As life goes, business took her family to a foreign country-a place called Moab. But even in that distant land their family blossomed. Life was good. Then, without even the faintest hint that heartbreak was standing at her door, Naomi's husband didn't return home for dinner. Who could have known that their kiss that morning would have been their last? Her sons eventually married, but even their weddings and talk of children couldn't take away the emptiness she felt. Finally, in a cruel twist that even Hollywood wouldn't script, she lost both of her sons. She was devastated, alone and bewildered. Naomi was so broken that Ruth 1:20 tells us that she began asking people to not call her Naomi (meaning 'pleasant') anymore but Mara (meaning 'bitter').*
>
> *The bright spot, if there can be a bright spot in someone's tragic loss, is that there was someone who didn't leave her. Her name was Ruth, her daughter-in-law. We're told she didn't offer any deep theological explanations. There's no record that she tried to provide the "right word" at the "right time." All we hear is*

Ruth's promise in Ruth 1:16, 'Where you go I will go, and where you stay, I will stay.' And that's exactly what she did."

~Brian Jones

Not only did Ruth realize Naomi needed her, my personal belief (a non-inspired Tara-ism) is that Ruth needed Naomi just as deeply. In fact, Ruth 1:14 states that she 'clung' to Naomi.

Everyone grieves in different ways: some need lots of time alone. Others need to be surrounded by loved ones. There is no right or wrong in grieving. Just make sure that the people you have surrounding you during your time of loss will point you towards Christ. He is the Great Physician.

Because of Ruth's devotion, God blessed her greatly with a new husband who provided for both her and Naomi; in addition, Ruth became the great-grandmother of King David, placing her as one of the great women in the lineage of Christ. Her condition at the start of the story was not her conclusion.

Jesus

The greatest example in dealing with grief is our Savior; the God-man who Isaiah stated was "a man of sorrows and familiar with suffering" (Isaiah 53:3)

He was wounded greatly while He was with us: not just physically, but emotionally as well. Zechariah 13:6 declares, "And one shall say unto him, What are these wounds in thine hands? Then he shall answer, Those with which I was wounded in the house of my friends."

One of the most telling passages of Jesus' sorrow is found in Matthew 26. He knows the agony and shame He would soon endure. Unimaginable pain, betrayal...the fate of the entire human race resting on his shoulders.

"Then Jesus went with his disciples to a place called Gethsemane, and he said to them, 'Sit here while I go over there and pray.' He took Peter and the two sons of Zebedee along with him, and he began to be sorrowful and troubled. Then he said to them, 'My soul is overwhelmed with sorrow to the point of death. Stay here and keep watch with me.'

Going a little farther, he fell with his face to the ground and prayed, 'My Father, if it is possible, may this cup be taken from me. Yet not as I will but as you will.'" (verses 36-39)

"Gethsemane" means 'oil press'. The pressure of His sacrifice was squeezing around Him. And I think it's interesting to note that Jesus' human part didn't want to suffer. His humanity didn't want to drink the cup of sorrow placed before Him. It's normal to want to pull away from grief. But I'm also glad that my Savior knows how we feel. He endured everything we have. He understands our pain and emotions. What a Savior!

Have you ever prayed, "Lord, get me out of this! I don't think I can bear it. Divorce...sickness...losing a child. Take this sorrow from me. Please take it away!"

But often, the cup remains.

The key to surviving, to understanding it, to living victoriously through it, is found in Jesus' plea. It should be the cry of all of our hearts. "Yet not as I will, but as you will." It is standing on faith that God is Who He says He is and that His plan is far better than my own.

"Then he returned to his disciples and found them sleeping. 'Could you men not keep watch with me for one hour?'...."

To add to His pain, His closest friends couldn't even stay awake and support him! Friendship is a wonderful thing, but our friends cannot always understand what dealing with intense grief is like. They want to help. They want to be there for you, but it's hard for them to understand how to give you what you need. The only person who can understand fully is the person who has lived through the same pain.

> *"He went away a second time and prayed, 'My Father, if it is not possible for this cup to be taken away unless I drink it, may your will be done.'*
>
> *When he came back, he again found them sleeping, because their eyes were heavy. So he left them and went away once more and prayed the third time, saying the same thing." (verses 42-44)*

Jesus' pain was intense; so heart breaking, in fact, the Bible says, "his sweat was like drops of blood falling to the ground" (Luke 22:44). This was bad enough, but He also had to endure the anguish of the cross. Spikes hammered through his hands and feet, whipped with a cat of nine tails, beaten, spat upon, hung naked on a tree while being mocked and verbally abused.

Separated from His Father while carrying our sin...my sin, He cried out, "My God, my God, why have you forsaken me?" I have heard it said that this moment was the darkest hour of history.

Yet, it didn't stay that way.

Jesus died, was buried but arose again on the third day! "Weeping may endure for a night, but joy comes in the morning." (Psalm 30:5) This sorrow, this time of weeping is painful but it will end. Maybe not all at once, but step by step. To some measure, it will occupy a room in your heart for a long time. We are never the same after tragedy strikes us. We get through it, but not over it.

Yet, there is healing available in Christ. "He has sent me to bind up the brokenhearted." (Isaiah 61:1) One of the meanings for the Hebrew word for "bind" in this passage is "to wrap around." The key to healing from grief is to surrender to God's master plan and let Christ wrap his pierced hands around your broken heart. He wants to share in your sufferings, to love on you...to hold you as you cry.

Grief Section 5: Rainbows and Rain... Learning to see the Good

"God is not the author of our comfort zone."
~ Lynn Rayburn

I Shall Know Him

The great hymn writer Fanny Crosby touched countless lives during her ministry and lifetime. She composed over 8,000 hymns, many that are still sung today. After being asked about her blindness since birth, Fanny said:

"It seemed intended by the blessed providence of God that I should be blind all my life, and I thank Him for the dispensation. If perfect earthly sight were offered me tomorrow I would not accept it. I might not have sung hymns to the praise of God if I had been distracted by the beautiful and interesting things about me…if I had a choice, I would still choose to remain blind…for when I die, the first face I will ever see will be the face of my blessed Savior."

Oh, that I could have her vision!
You see, Mrs. Crosby found the secret to contentment. And that comes when we know that God truly does have our best

in mind and that He is working all things together for our good, whether we understand it or not.

> *"All things work together for good to those who love God, to those who are the called according to his purpose."*
> ~Romans 8:28 (NKJV)

Consider the words of Jesus in John 9:

> *"As he went along, he saw a man blind from birth. His disciples asked him, 'Rabbi, who sinned, this man or his parents, that he was born blind?'*
>
> *'Neither this man nor his parents sinned,' said Jesus, 'but this happened so that the work of God might be displayed in his life'. Having said this, he spit on the ground, made some mud with the saliva, and put it on the man's eyes. 'Go', he told him, 'wash in the Pool of Siloam'...so the man went and washed, and came home seeing."*

The rest of John 9 goes on to tell that the news of the man's healing spread like wild-fire. The Pharisees cried in outrage that Jesus had healed on the Sabbath, but their reaction actually caused some people to believe in Jesus.

I'm sure this blind man had wondered many times, "Why me? Why can't I see like everyone else? What possible good can come out of a blind beggar?" But in God's perfect timing using His own Son, this man was healed and Jesus was glorified. As a result, this healing is now engraved in God's Word for eternity.

Water Balloons

My aunt is a horse expert. And she has used a tried and true technique to teach her horses not to rear.

She takes a water balloon (yes, you read that right), fills it with warm water and mounts into the saddle. Every time the horse tries to rear, she breaks the warm water balloon between the horses ears. The horse will quiet immediately. Why? The warm water makes him think he's bleeding and self preservation kicks in. When the horse thinks he is hurt (whether real or imagined) he gets still.

Aren't we the same way? Sometimes we don't calm down and look up until tragedy, whether real or perceived, strikes.

I've heard it said that people are like stained-glass windows. They sparkle and shine when the sun is out, but when the darkness sets in, their true beauty is revealed only if there is a light from within. What a beautiful picture! "My grace is sufficient for you, for my power is made perfect in weakness." (2 Corinthians 12:9) Without brokenness, God's glory cannot be fully displayed.

My prayer is that we will know God's presence, even when we do not understand his ways.

"He will wipe away every tear from their eyes, and death shall be no more, neither shall there be mourning, nor crying, nor pain anymore, for the former things have passed away."
~Psalm 147:3 (ESV)

Oh, my friend, though this landmine bring great sadness, I pray that you will be comforted in knowing that your Savior has not abandoned you on the battlefield. Indeed, He is picking you up and carrying you home.

The Wound

If you've been struggling with grief, a vital part, and necessary first step, to healing is to discover your wound. (Remember what we discussed in *Finding the Wound* on page 16.)

What is the wound you received that created your grief in the first place? Search your heart. What is the source of your pain? If you can identify that, (for some it may be easy and for others it may be difficult), you can confront it.

For some, it may be the missing what was lost. For others, it might be anger at God, grieving a strained relationship that never had a chance to heal or the inability to let go.

Cry the necessary tears you need to shed for the loss. Let those emotions and hurts roll over you so healing can begin. Embrace it and absorb it.

This is the first step to disarming the landmine of grief, and consequently, being free from it. Then, in time, you may learn to see the big picture in the suffering. You'll learn to see the good and cling to God's promises of hope. Eventually, that open wound will heal. A scar may be left behind, but it will be a reminder of how far you've come in God's strength.

LANDMINE #2: DEPRESSION

"For me being depressed means you can spend all day in bed, and still not get a good night's rest."
~ Unknown

"Depression is like living in shades of gray."
~ Anonymous

"If depression is creeping up and must be faced, learn something about the nature of the beast: You may escape without a mauling."
~ Dr. R.W. Shepherd

"Me, depressed? But I'm a comedian. ... I have to get back to work! I have jokes to write. How can I write a joke when I'm depressed? Will it sound like this?: 'Knock-knock. Go away!'"
~ Chonda Pierce

Okay. We are going there. Yep, we are gonna talk about it. Depression. And I apologize if it sounds, well, depressing.

To be honest, I've had a very hard time trying to approach this subject. It's so weighty. It's so consuming. Maybe I'm scared I will write something that leads someone in the wrong direction. Or maybe I am not finished wrestling out my own issues with this subject. Maybe it's because I tend to be an optimistic person and I want to run from darkness and talk of weighty matters. Give me light-hearted banter, jokes and joy any day.

But really, isn't that the very reason that depression is what it is? No one likes it. Nobody wants to have to fight with every fiber of their being just to be able to get up out of bed. Nobody wants to feel like they are drowning.

Depression is the unexpected landmine that keeps on exploding. It's the nightmare that keeps on giving. Don't get me wrong. I'm not talking about 'feeling a little blue' or about 'being in a funk'. I'm talking about soul-deep depression. The type that leaves you breathless and desperate for just one ray of light.

Chonda Pierce describes depression this way: like walking around with a heavy weight on your head and shoulders and wearing dark sunglasses nonstop. For me, it was feeling so overwhelmed and crushed in spirit that I just wanted to escape. Didn't care when or how.

In short, depression leaves it's victim feeling like the shell of the person they once were: hollow.

I Was The Poster Child...

"That is depression, that force of trying to hold your head up and trying to see the world on a sunny day but to you it just seems dark and cloudy. That is what depression feels like on a good day. On a bad day, you don't even want to get out of bed." ~ Unknown

Some of you reading this may already know my story. Some may not. Let me just say that back in 2002, I had the worst year of my life. Depression hit my body hard and heavy. I will get into the reasons why in just a little bit, but suffice to say, I never, *ever* want to return to that place again.

I'd heard about depression all of my life, but you know, sometimes something just doesn't click until it hits you personally. Looking back I can see the signs so easily: weight gain, lack of concentration, lack of focus…I was like a Chihuahua! It didn't matter how deeply I set my mind to do something, my ability to focus fluttered around like a moth on crack.

Not that I was hyper, by any means. I remember having to force myself out of bed. It wasn't that I was melancholy or just wanted some extra 'down time'. It literally took every amount of grit and determination I had just to rise in the morning. It's odd because at first, it just felt like "Man, I'm really tired tonight." Follow that up with day after day of feeling 'really tired'. Before too long, seven or eight hours of sleep wouldn't do. Then it's nine hours, ten hours….and the more I slept, the more exhausted I became.

All I could think of was, 'When can I crawl back into bed?" I went to my classes at UALR, ate my meals, worked in the music department, went to church…but every night I would collapse into bed, mentally begging those cool sheets to relieve me of my exhaustion.

And when you're that exhausted and strung out, nothing sounds like fun. I couldn't laugh and joke. Concentrating on having fun took too much effort. Things that I had loved to do before like reading, writing, singing, playing piano or painting held absolutely no interest for me. Everything was bland. There was no color and no sparks.

But most of all I just wanted to escape…leave all my responsibilities behind and run. And I didn't know how.

Symptoms

I have talked to many people over the past few years who have battled this, and here are other symptoms that they experienced:

- **Insomnia** — some of them could only sleep about one hour a night
- **Weight loss or gain**

- **Non stop crying for no apparent reason**
- **Detachment from loved ones**
- **A feeling of numbness**
- **Inability to concentrate**
- **Nervousness**
- **Pondering suicide**
- **Panic attacks**
- **Outbursts of anger** (particularly in men)
- **Overwhelming feelings of sadness**
- **Feeling abandoned by God**

Now, I'm going to stop right here for a minute and tell you that when I was diagnosed with depression, I said "Uh-uh. No way. I'm a Christian and Christians aren't supposed to get depressed." Well, let's look at that for a moment, shall we?

Living Victorious....Right?

When my doctor told me I was depressed, I almost did a spit-take. Me? Miss Has-it-together-preacher's-kid-Pollyanna-wanna-be-who-loves-Jesus? Not possible.

But, in fact, I *was* depressed. I couldn't escape that fact and it seemed at war with everything I had known and had been taught in churches for years. If you love and trust Jesus, you will live victoriously....right?

Victorious over death....yes. Victorious over Satan...yes. Jesus gives us many victories and of course the ultimate is His victory over the grave. But He never promised we wouldn't go through some hard stuff. We live in a fallen world with fallen, frail bodies. The touch of sin is everywhere and we will have to deal with it until He comes again to give us our new glorified bodies. (By the way, mine will be a size 2.) He never said we wouldn't deal with some rough stuff. He just promised to be there for us no matter what comes. Contrary to popular opinion, this truly isn't our best life now. That will only come in Heaven.

In the meantime, we have to deal with death, disease, cancer, bad eye sight, bad hearts, diabetes and yes, even depression. You see, I fell into the mentality that says "If you're depressed, you aren't close to Jesus. You don't love Him enough." Don't ever fall for that…that is a lie straight from the pits of hell! I have heard many well-intentioned Christians say this and it makes me want to pull my hair out. Pardon my bluntness…

Let's look at King David. He penned psalm after psalm, many of them crying out in his despair. This guy was dealing with tough stuff.

"Give me relief from my distress…"
~ Psalms 4:1

"Heal me, for my bones are in agony. My soul is in anguish. How long, O LORD, how long?...I am worn out from groaning; all night long I flood my bed with weeping and drench my couch with tears."
~ Psalms 6

"How long, O LORD? Will you forget me forever? How long will you hide Your face from me?...
How long must I wrestle with my thoughts and every day have sorrow in my heart?"
~ Psalms 13

"The cords of death entangled me; the torrents of destruction overwhelmed me. The cords of the grave coiled around me; the snares of death confronted me."
~Psalms 18:4,5

Yet, look at David's continuation to these cries.

"I lie down and sleep; I wake again, because the LORD sustains me."
~ Psalms 3:5

"The Lord has heard my cry for mercy."
~ Psalms 6:9

"But I trust in Your unfailing love…"
~ Psalms 13

"Keep me as the apple of your eye; hide me in the shadow of Your wings."
~Psalms 17:8

"I love you, O LORD, my strength."
~Psalms 18:1

"In my distress I called to the LORD…from his temple He heard my voice…
He drew me out of deep waters."
~Psalms 18

"You turned my wailing into dancing."
~Psalms 30:11

You see, the focus isn't on whether David should or should not have been depressed. We feel what we feel. But what is important is *who* he cried to for help. The Lord of Lords, King of Kings, Creator, Jehovah. God called David a man after His own heart, not because he always had it together and did everything right, but because David continually turned to the Lord in moments of joy and in despair.

Please, Somebody tell me why!

"I know God will not give me anything I can't handle. I just wish that He didn't trust me so much."
~Mother Teresa

So what causes depression? I wish there were a simple answer to that. A simple answer would mean a simple solution. The reasons are varied from person to person and often take many, many years to figure out.

Remember that core wound we've talked about? This is a great place to reflect if you're not sure what has caused your depression. Many people argue that a lot of depression issues are related to our wound at it's foundation and then is just rekindled by the problems listed below. However, it's different for each person. As we study through these things, remember the goal is to deactivate the landmine.

Here are just a few possible causes:

- **traumatic life changes like death, divorce, etc.**
- **genetics**
- **hormonal changes**
- **high levels of stress and/or conflict**
- **abuse- past physical, sexual or emotional abuse**
- **certain medications**
- **prolonged physical illness**
- **Post traumatic stress disorder**
- **un-confessed sin or prolonged sin issues**
- **perfectionism**
- **people-pleasing**

This is just scratching the surface. Depression is usually highly complex and multi-faceted. And yes, sometimes there might not be any explainable reason. Chemicals in the brain don't function like they used to and depression forms. Be careful not to judge or analyze someone suffering from depression. There might not be a discernable cause.

Speaking for myself, my own depression was a result of being a perfectionist and people-pleaser, eventually working myself into such an exhausted state that the serotonin in my brain was depleted. I became so fixated on keeping everyone happy, that I lost sight of my Savior. Jesus' burdens are light. Man's are much heavier. I was physically unable to function anymore.

One night in 2002, something inside me snapped. The landmine exploded. I lay on the bathroom floor sobbing until three a.m. The main thing that I remember was feeling like I was drowning. I couldn't breathe. Couldn't escape. And with every fiber of my being, that is what I wanted…to escape.

If you are currently suffering from depression, don't give up! There is hope! Let's take a look at section 2.

Depression Section 2: Finding Summertime Again

"In the midst of winter, I finally learned that there was in me an invincible summer."

~Albert Camus

If you are reading this and are currently fighting the crashing waves of depression, I want you to know that there is hope. I promise. I've been there. God loves you far beyond what you can even imagine and He has only good and beautiful things planned for your life. The enemy will try to trick you into believing the lie "Life is sad and over and done and you'll never get out of this". Don't believe it! I have come out on the other side and I can tell you my walk with God is so much stronger for having survived it.

Depression is treatable. Below I've listed advice from friends and acquaintances who have battled this illness and won.

1. **Seek medical attention.** Depression usually results from a chemical imbalance. It takes an extremely long time for these chemicals to replenish, if at all. It just depends on the person and the reason. Medication will help give you relief from the symptoms while you work on finding the cause.

Okay, before we move on let me say that I know taking medication is not a popular thing in the Christian world. And I am probably going to hear about this later. A friend of mine put it this way: "There doesn't seem to be much stigma among Christians about *having* depression; the fuss seems to be about taking medication for it." I have noted this to be very true. And for the life of me, I don't know why. Whenever I hear someone fussing about this, I just scratch my head in wonder.

If a person has diabetes, don't they take insulin? If someone's heart is weak, don't they swallow pills to keep themselves from having a heart attack? And if your eyes are bad, don't you wear glasses? Depression is no different. There is something chemically wrong that needs to be fixed. You still have to try to find the reason behind it, but in the meantime, those chemicals desperately need to be replaced. This is just one tool God has given us to help. There are also herbal remedies and a host of other things that I haven't even mentioned.

2. **Seek counseling with a trusted Christian counselor**. I stress the word 'christian'. It is incredibly important that the person trying to help you dig to the core of who you are is a follower of Christ. It is God who ultimately does the revealing and healing.

3. **Listen to upbeat praise and worship music.**

4. **Pray**. Even if it is hard to form the words to pray, just cry out to God. He hears His children.

5. **Share what is going on with someone you trust**. But make sure the person is 'safe'. A safe person is not one who will immediately condemn you. This is a person who will listen, be there for you, and speak the truth in love. Confiding in an unsafe person will only deepen your feelings of

hopelessness.

6. ***If you can, read your Bible***. This is often hard for some people in the middle of this storm. I had a friend who battled this and she was physically unable to read. Her eyes blurred and she couldn't concentrate on a single sentence. That's okay. Get the Bible on CD. The Word of Promise is a great one. Even if you are in your bed, let it play and soak it in.

7. ***Make small goals***. Some people have functional depression. They can get up, go to work, take care of their kids but collapse into bed later. Some are completely unable to rise from bed. In this scenario, it's especially important to take your recovery slow but steady. For starters, make a victory journal. Jot down any progress. Even if you are only able to rise out of bed for 30 minutes and move to a different room, that is a victory! Write it down. Work a puzzle. Do a load of laundry. Go to a movie. These may seem small but they are monumental in helping you reclaim the life God intended you to have.

During my own recovery time I read a lot. My doctor introduced me to some wonderful Christian writers named Henry Cloud and John Townsend. Their book *Boundaries* was life changing for me. They have many others: *Safe People*, and *Changes That Heal* are just two. Go to a Christian bookstore and look around.

The best advice I was given was to do an intense study of Jesus: not just His teachings, but how He interacted with people. Did he take time away? Was He always nice? In doing so, I realized that Jesus is not a people pleaser. He is a God pleaser. This realization helped me jump over a big hurdle. Because if I'm supposed to be imitating Jesus, that means that I should only live to please God and not every one else. A huge burden lifted off of me. I didn't have to work so hard and exhaust myself. I found freedom. God's love is unconditional! I discovered *that* was the source of my depression: I was exhausting myself to find unconditional love in conditional people. (Remember the wound I talked about in the introduction? Depression was the landmine and my wound was needing to feel loved.)

Lost At Sea

To understand this more deeply, I've included the scenario that I share with audiences whenever I am allowed the opportunity to speak or sing for churches and other events. I make the audience close their eyes and try to put themselves directly into the middle of this story. This account is the core of my wound.

> *Imagine you are in the middle of a stormy sea. It's dark; you can barely see your hand in front of your face. Thunder is crashing. Rain is slicing like bullets in your skin. A furious wind whips the waves into a psychotic frenzy and the only light visible is from the strikes of lightening overhead which just add to your terror.*
>
> *You realize you are alone in the middle of the stormy sea and unless you swim to land, you'll drown. So you begin to swim, but the waves keep beating you back. You work harder and harder but can't seem to make any headway.*
>
> *In the middle of the storm's chaos, you begin to hear voices telling to kick to the right. Another voice is screaming to head to the left. Another voice, screaming louder than all the others tells you to give up. It's a hopeless cause and you are sure to drown. Your muscles begin to ache from exertion. Your lungs are filling up with water and you're having trouble staying focused on surviving. You can't catch your breath. You begin thinking about everyone who is depending on you: your family, children, church, friends. You keep struggling but begin to feel yourself sinking.*
>
> *You're so tired and can't go on. In your anguish and terror, you cry to God, "I need You!". But it's useless. You succumb to sinking into the depths.*

You prepare to feel the sensation of falling, but realize something is holding you up above water. With a start, you notice that the storm doesn't look as ferocious as it did mere moments ago. You look down into water and see a ring of light around your body. The reflection is so beautiful as it shimmers against the water's surface.

Sucking in a surprised breath, you notice someone has an arm around your waist. You turn your head around to see who is holding you up. Your eyes meet the eyes of Jesus and He is smiling at you in love and peace.

You say, "Lord, where were you? I have been fighting for my life out here! Where have you been in the middle of this storm?"

He levels his gaze into your eyes and says, "My arms have been around you the whole time. Why were you fighting so hard? I've done all the work for you already. You just need to trust Me and hold on tight."

You're shocked to realize you've been working so hard for nothing. You let the voices and your fear take your focus off of Christ. Your muscles relax and rest knowing that He is leading out of the storm. At the same time, you feel foolish for listening to those screaming voices. You remember that Christ has never let you fall.

H.A.L.T!

Halt is a great way to remember to take care of yourself. And that is something that is very, very important. HALT stands for: don't let yourself get *hungry, angry, lonely or tired*. If you leave yourself vulnerable to these things, it's a very quick spiral down again. If you're a tad bit tired, don't ignore it. Get some extra rest. Don't run around all day skipping meals. This will wreak havoc with your body. Be aware if you are pushing people away---that will make you more vulnerable to satanic attack. It's important to be proactive.

And, yes, it's possible that your depression will come back again. But you know what? If it does, it does. At least you'll be better equipped, better prepared, wiser and stronger than you were before. I've had two smaller bouts of depression since 2002 and they were less intense than the first time because I knew the tools God gave me. I was familiar with them. I understood my body much better. I understood my relationship with God better.

Here's the thing about depression: *you cannot operate based on how you feel. You have to cling to what you know.* I think the most terrifying thing for me was feeling so far from God. I was numb. I couldn't sense Him with me. Just like King David, I felt like I had been abandoned. But He was there with me the whole time. I had to keep reminding myself of His promises.

This is why it's critical to nurture your relationship with God. Stay close to Him. If you drift, you will leave yourself open to much deeper heartache. You may not always feel like praying or reading your Bible, but do it anyways. You won't regret it. Looking back, I know that Jesus was the only reason I made it through.

DEPRESSION SECTION 3: BEING THE HANDS OF JESUS

"Whenever someone sorrows, I do not say, "forget it," or "it will pass," or "it could be worse" — all of which deny the integrity of the painful experience."
~Peter Koenstenbaum

So maybe you are reading this and thinking, "Hey, this ain't me! I've never been depressed." That's wonderful and I pray you never are. But there is still something to learn here, because it's likely that someone you love may end up going through this exact situation someday. And as the saying goes, you can be the hands and feet of Jesus to them when they need Him most.

Helping someone with depression requires patience and tact. Chonda Pierce recently stated, "The best way people can reach out to loved ones dealing with depression is to just be there for them and realize they can not pull the person out of it on their own. Allow them to feel what they are feeling."

It's especially tough in church. Don't get me wrong. Most of the time, your brothers and sisters in Christ mean well. They desperately want you to feel better. They want to see that pep in your step and your smile back. Oftentimes, they just don't know what to say. And if someone hasn't been through it, they simply don't understand.

Don't give advice if you haven't been through it yourself. Don't accuse. Don't try to do psychoanalysis on them. Just love them. That's what they need. Try not to be hurt if they push you away. That's part of depression. It's like telling a child "Don't crave candy". Be gentle, sensitive and patient. Depression usually doesn't hit overnight, and so it won't be healed overnight. It takes time.

Don't try to reassure them by saying things like "You shouldn't feel that way…" or the like. This only tends to compound the depressed person's guilt and isolation. Lots of TLC is required. And if they begin saying things like, "I just want to end it all" or "I shouldn't be in this world", don't brush it off. Those are very serious cries for help.

Be careful with the spiritual encouragement you might give. Although well intentioned, it can be painful. Implying that by simply sharing a scripture with a depressed person should be all the help they need to recover could only cause more hurt. Depressed people tend to think, "What's wrong with me? I know that the scripture my friend is sharing is from you, Lord, so why don't I feel better? I don't get any comfort from it. Am I a terrible Christian?" Guilt begins to build.

> *"What if we finally got the nerve to climb out of bed in the midst of our depression or our struggles in life, and we placed on the garments (tools) that God gave us? We took the medicine. We went to the counseling. We were studying. We were keeping in the Word. We were playing our praise music. We were doing everything we knew to do. And finally, in that heap of shame that we are in, we make our way into a church and the first thing that happens is someone looks at you and says, 'Now where is your faith? You take off that garment and believe in God!' when it was the God of the universe that provided that (those tools) in the first place."*

~ Chonda Pierce

You'll never go wrong by just listening. Bringing flowers. Reading the Bible to them when they can't rise. Praying over them. I distinctly remember every single person who listened and were patient with me when I was at my worst. Their love was like a lifeline when I felt like I was drowning.

Whether struggling with this issue or not, always remember that Jesus loves you. He loves you so much that He died for you. He wants your life to be full and joyous. And He will walk with you over every mountain and through every valley.

DEPRESSION SECTION 4:
BUT DON'T TAKE MY WORD FOR IT...

Depression has many faces. I faced my own battle with it and I will never, ever forget that feeling of drowning…of despair…of hopelessness.

As I have tried to reach out and help others battling the same problem, I've discovered that depression comes in many different forms and masks. I thought, "How can I help others when the problem can be so multi-faceted?" I figure a good start is to begin asking questions of those who have battled it and overcome it successfully. Not that depression can wholly be 'fixed'. Until the Lord comes back, we might have to deal with this issue many times over.

But there is hope! I recently asked a friend of mine to sit down with me and share her personal story. For the sake of her kids and church, she has asked to remain anonymous. She came to my house one sunshiny morning in March. She poured out her story while we sipped tea and played with my dog.

I pray her story blesses you as much as it did me...

So how old were you when you gave your life to Christ?

I was twenty two. It's funny: growing up my family really didn't pursue God, but I ended up visiting almost every single denomination out there. I wasn't really searching for God. I just went whenever my friends asked me to tag along with them. *(laughs)* I remember thinking that Christians were nuts! Now I am one. *(smiles)*

You're married with two children, and I know from talking with you that you are super involved in your church. What leadership positions do you hold?

I teach the ladies Bible study, am usually Vacation Bible School director, I teach in Vacation Bible School and am the Wednesday night youth leader.

You help with music too, don't you?

Oh yeah, that too. My husband is a deacon and I sometimes teach classes on Sunday morning as well.

I've heard it said that 20 percent of the church membership usually ends up doing 80 percent of the work. Do you agree with that statement?

Yes, only I think that number may be more drastic than that. Often it feels like 10 percent are doing 90 percent of the work.

So, I know from talking with you previously that you've battled depression.

Yes, several times actually.

Tell me about how it all started.

Well, the first time I struggled with it was right after my second child was born. I had postpartum depression but didn't even realize it because my son was so ill during the first two years. He was constantly in and out of the hospital and I didn't have time to analyze my feelings, emotions or energy. I just kept going on auto pilot. After the storm passed, I began to notice changes.

What changes?

My world revolved around my babies…always had. But I began to hide from them. I remember not wanting to play with them, just wanting to stay in bed all day. I couldn't deal with the responsibility of being a mom. I don't really remember much else.

It's a fog, isn't it?

Yes. My husband noticed those changes too and insisted that I go to the doctor. He put me on Zoloft and told me to give it six weeks to work.

Did it help?

Yeah, baby! (*laughs*) After just three days I told my husband, "I don't know what this stuff is, but it's goooooooood stuff!" I was extremely hyper. The only problem was that it made me so stinkin' hungry all the time. I gained a lot of weight. I felt better depression-wise, but was really upset by the weight gain. So I went off the Zoloft and switched to St. John's wort. It helped quite a bit.

Did anyone, friends, or church family know what you were going through?

The only people who knew were my husband and mom. I refused to share it with anybody at church.

Depression made me feel…..broken. And you know, Christians aren't supposed to be broken. I felt so inferior. I didn't want anyone to know and no one else in church talked about stuff like that. Plus I had a close friend who had dealt with depression before but she really turned me off of sharing with her.

How so?

Well, she blamed EVERYTHING on depression. She was always complaining about it. It really made me realize that I didn't want to be like her. I couldn't even have an 'off' day because she would automatically tell me it was depression. Not every Monday or bad day is caused by depression.

That's very true!

Whatever feelings she was having, she would reflect on to me. She kind of choked me on 'depression'.

That sounds like a projection problem. She took her own problems and projected them on to you to see what she wanted to see.

Yep. She gagged me on it. I didn't want to be like her so I just kept it bottled up.

Do you think your church family would have had issue with you sharing your battle with depression?

(thinks for a moment) I don't know. Probably not, but I'm not sure.

So you said that you've dealt with depression more than once. When did it come back?

Yeah, it came back in 2008. And it's odd because the symptoms were different, maybe because I was at a different stage in my life. There was a lot going on at that time.

What do you think caused it?

(takes a big breath) Too much. Everything happened like dominoes. We had several deaths in the family that left us kind of breathless. We changed churches. I was homeschooling, which was a big stresser. The responsibility for my kids' education fell squarely on my shoulders.

We have our own business and when the economy crashed, our business almost failed. We had to let most of our employees go because we couldn't afford to pay them. We had no paychecks and no money. We took on raising our nephew who was going through some bad family problems. And in the middle of all of that, we were building our house.

Good grief! Those are like the highest levels of stress known to man, all thrown into one pot!

(laughs) Tell me about it. And you have to understand, I was a super control freak. Like, I didn't make plans a month in advance…I made them six months to a year in advance! I wanted control and security. If my little home nest was secure, I was good. And all of a sudden, I was pulled out of my comfort zone by my nails and teeth.

Are you adaptable to change now?

Now? Sure. I definitely wasn't then. All that stress had a way of breaking me into someone different.

Everything kind of snowballed. I remember one January morning, in the midst of all this craziness, I woke up, took the kids to school (because we had finally enrolled them in a school down the road), came home, walked into the bedroom, shut the door, curled up on the floor and bawled my eyes out. I just snapped.

I had just gotten a part time job to try to help supplement our income during the financial crisis. I laid there sobbing and just kept thinking, "I can't go to work. I can't face anybody." I was petrified. I wondered if I was going insane or something. I knew I needed something- therapy, counseling, medicine…but didn't know what.

I was so petrified and was scared to be alone. I called my husband at work and he came to pick me up. He drove me around with him all day, just so I wouldn't be alone. I took my Bible with me in the truck. I tried to read it, but it was so weird. I couldn't understand it. It was like reading a different language or something. I couldn't concentrate.

And isn't that a scary feeling?

Absolutely! It's like there is no light or color. Everything is just black. The most terrifying thing was that I just couldn't find God. I knew He was there but I couldn't feel Him or hear Him. I couldn't sense Him with me at all.

I remember telling my husband that I needed help but didn't know what to do. I said "I need you to help me get help." Does that make sense? (*laughs*)

(I laugh.) I understand that completely. In the midst of all that, a person just wants hope and needs to have their feet placed to take a step in the right direction.

And it's really neat how God worked. One of my husband's customers at the store is a counselor. They got me set up for a visit, but I didn't want to talk to a man. I don't know why. And with us having no money, that was another stress. I didn't want my counseling sessions to bankrupt us.

We found a counseling center that fits the payments to the patients' financial situations, so God worked that one out.

Did you go see a female counselor?

Yes, but looking back, I wish I had talked to the male counselor we had originally met. The woman counselor I went to needed counseling herself! *(laughs)*

Oh no! That doesn't help, huh?

I remembered that several of our sessions turned into her asking *me* for advice. And part of it was my fault. I had no patience with counseling. I just wanted everything ripped off like a band-aid and to be 'fixed' right away. Counseling doesn't work that way.

But she gave me some really great relaxation techniques to help with my insomnia. It didn't fix things but it gave me some great starter tools.

So how did you end up turning the corner?

I ended up going back to my medical doctor. He put me on Celexa. At first the dosage was too high and it put me in a zombie state, but we got it adjusted and the difference is amazing!

What sort of changes did you notice?

I could concentrate again and read my Bible. I wasn't crying nearly as much. Just being able to read and concentrate gave me a lot of hope that things would continue to get better.

What advice would you give to people suffering from depression?

Get help! Go to a medical doctor *first*, and then go to a counselor if you need help figuring out 'why' you are depressed. Medicine can provide a lot of relief while trying to figure out the causes.

Medicine was essential in my own recovery. It replenishes the serotonin and brings you back into the land of the living again.

Yep. And it's really interesting because people in my own church, several years later now are much more open than they used to be, and I think it's because with my last bout of depression, I just decided I was going to be incredibly vulnerable and honest. God pretty much told me to stop hiding. He spoke to my heart. "You are not my first child to deal with it and you won't be the last."

Stop right there. That's actually a pretty profound thought.

Well, I didn't tell *everyone* right away. I started by telling a few more trusted women in the church and they were very open to hearing and understanding. But I've noticed the stigma doesn't seem to be with *having* depression, but instead having to take medication for it.

What techniques did the counselor give you that helped?

Oh, basic relaxation techniques mostly. I physically could not relax in any way when I was at my worst. She recommended exercise.

That's a bigee for me.

Me too. Even simple things like taking a warm bath before bed helps. Get the water as hot as you can stand it. It really did help my insomnia.

It takes courage to knock down those walls. And as long as it is hidden, our enemy uses it to keep us locked up in fear. We don't live up to our potential in Christ when that's the case.

Yeah, I just decided to be more vocal about it. Satan no longer has any power over me in that. By living in shame, I was tying God's hands as to what He could use to glorify Him.

And really, it took all of that craziness to get me malleable to change and God's will.

~ ~ ~

Here are more thoughts from another friend:

Interview Segment with Dominic

Have you ever struggled with depression?

Oh yes! I have PTSD [*Post Traumatic Stress Disorder*] from Vietnam. I don't think that I've slept more than four hours a stretch for the past forty years.

What were the symptoms?

Well, I didn't even know I had it for a while. Big groups tend to make me nervous. When I feel nervous, uncontrollable, violent reactions come out. I couldn't keep a job. If I felt like I might get violent during a confrontation, I would run away. I knew I had little control over my body and was scared to death I might attack. It's that whole fight or flight thing. Since Vietnam I have become a highly suspicious person... suspicious of others, assuming the worst about them.

How were you able to take steps to overcome?

Counseling for years and years and years. I can recognize the symptoms now and have the tools to help. Going through all that...it almost killed me. I still carry the scars. It's so easy for me to slip into combat mode. One night my wife thought she would prank me while I was sleeping. She crept in the bed and began shaking me, giggling and trying to scare me. The next thing I knew she was slammed into the wall with a shiner and I was sitting upright with my fists clenched. I had punched her before I even knew what was going on. Talk about feeling terrible!

(*Smile*) I bet she never pranked you again.

(laughs) Nope.

~ ~ ~

Hang with me here, my friend. There are still several more interviews to go. But I think it's important to understand just how differently depression can manifest itself and what a wide range of people it affects.

Interview Segment with Scott

When did your illness start?

It's been a long term thing that began from being exposed to mold in my classroom. After several years of that, my immune system went nuts and I began having severe inflammation before a nasty virus set in. I was getting no sleep…none. My bowels shut down. I could go into more detail but I'll spare you. *(laughs)* Doctors didn't know what to do with me. And then I began having severe reactions to any drugs they gave me. It took four to five years before I started getting answers to what was wrong.

One doctor finally got a handle on it and labeled it Chronic Inflammatory Response Syndrome. My nervous system buzzes all the time and I'm allergic to *everything*, especially what I consume. Often times the allergic reactions are explosive. At one point early on in the illness, I lost fifty pounds.

I know the feeling of going doctor to doctor and the frustration when no one knows what the problem is.

Well, after a while they begin telling you that it's all in your head. If you have three or more symptoms, they label you a psychiatric basket case. *(laughs)* It's so hard for them to say, 'I don't know', so they reason it must be a mental disorder.

Which only makes the frustration and isolation so much worse. Did this prolonged illness cause any depression? I can't imagine it NOT causing depression!

Oh yes! Some of it was from the illness, some from lack of sleep and some of it from my family not understanding what I was going through and not wanting to understand.

Can you describe for me how you felt, what went through your mind when the depression was at its worst?

(Searches for words) It's all so....all encompassing. When my pain level went up I would become more irritable, more agitated, which pushed those around me away. As a result, they didn't want to have anything to do with me. I had three very dear friends and I can honestly say that if it weren't for them, I wouldn't be here today.

And since I couldn't sleep, they stacked me on lots of sleep medications which only made the depression worse.

I've heard it said that depressed women tend to cry more and depressed men tend to have more trouble with irritation and anger.

Well, I cried too. For a while there, I was crying all the time. When I got sick, my kids were just five and three. They don't ever remember me being healthy. It's odd because my oldest child is slightly autistic and has seemed to weather it better. But my youngest child won't have anything to do with me. And it breaks my heart…every single day.

How did you make it through that?

Well, after a while I found a doctor who knew that something was, as he put it, 'irritating the devil' out of my nervous system. Just having him understand made a huge difference, even if he didn't have the answers.

Wow. That's actually a very profound statement. It's all about empathy and compassion and not necessarily about finding out the 'whys'.

When we began piecing together what had happened, the doctor gave me some great brochures to read about what was going on with me, medically and otherwise. None of my family would read them. They just wanted to know if it could be 'fixed'.

I would try to share what was going on but my family didn't want to hear it, which made me turn inward and made me more miserable.

I'll say this: when going through a prolonged illness, you learn who your true friends are. And for me, they were only the friends who had gone through some long term suffering themselves.

It's a constant battle within me. "Should I share the medical facts with them to help them understand or do I just walk away?" *(laughs)* Neither option helps. And I've told them, "You are judging something you don't understand."

What advice would you give someone going through this exact problem?

Learn who your real friends are. It won't be a quick thing, but a long drawn-out process. And don't just find friends who will listen to *you*, but also share similar interests. Go out and do things together. Build a relationship.

Also counseling is good. Having a paid friend who will listen is helpful. To be honest, a deep regular friendship is more beneficial, but counseling does help a bit. When the doors were shutting and my walls were closing in, my true friends were actually more helpful, and awesome, than any counselor.

True friends, ones who are willing to speak the truth in love, but *continue* to love you, even when it's hard and unpleasant are truly rare.

(Laughs) The best friends will hear what I'm saying but not give me much of a response on 'what to do', which is actually a good thing! *(smiles)* The amazing thing is that they listened without condemning me, but when the tables turned and they were going through their own rough time, they began to lean on me. That love, being needed, is another form of therapy.

It's good to be needed and wanted. That is the most powerful part of healing.

To be honest, I feel trapped in my own family. And when my illness was wreaking havoc, my family actually asked me to leave at one point. They didn't want to deal with it. I don't ever feel needed or wanted with them.

One of my best friends who is a pastor told me once, "Scott, Jesus' own hometown rejected him." And that seems to be the way of it sometimes. Those who are closest to you, are often the first to push you away.

~ ~ ~

Interview Segment with Kerrie

Have you ever struggled with depression?

I had one big round with that. I think anyone will tell you that I'm a pretty happy person, but in 2003, we were having church problems, Mark's mom was in the hospital dying, my friend Mary Lee was dying and to top it all off, my dog died!

It felt like a black hole. I *never* want to go back there again.

One night I was crying to Mark and he stopped me and said, "Kerrie, can you control any of this?" I couldn't it. And it was just like a slap across the face. I thought, "What am I doing? I can't fix any of this."

I'd been feeling like there was a black curtain over my head. I cried all the time and slept all the time. I would go to town and think, "Can't everyone see how miserable I am?" I had a big old pity party.

My depression lasted about four months. What helped the most was that chat with Mark. It was like a cold washrag hit me. There was a new awareness that some things were just out of my hands. The next day I got my gumption back. I determined to have the grit to fight and pull myself up by my bootstraps.

Did you ever take any medicine?

I went all natural and used Evening primrose. I tell everyone about it! It takes the edge off. I really didn't want medicine because my sister was put on Prozac and she ended up sleeping her life away. I didn't want to live like that. But hey, after going through depression, I realized why some people need it. There is definitely no shame in using medicine.

~ ~ ~

Interview Segment with Nan

Since I've retired, I spend half my day reading the Bible. When that depression tries to sneak back, I do extra Bible reading. To get any healing, you have to realize you are depressed.

Get an accountability partner; someone who will keep your confidence. Be a good listener and a trustworthy friend.

Don't keep your feelings bottled up. Scream, stomp, yell--- whatever you need to do, but get it out! And keep a journal. Write your feelings down.

~ ~ ~

And now I'd like to introduce you to my dear friend, Kathy. Years ago, Kathy's son was in jail and went through some very turbulent years. From age eight and on, he was constantly in trouble. Kathy courageously shares part of her journey below...

Interview with Kathy

When things were bad with him, I just wanted to hide from everybody...church, business...everything.

And look at your son now. A minister, youth pastor...I absolute adore him!

(smiles) Well that was part of his problem growing up...he was so likeable that it kept him from getting into much trouble when he was younger. But later on, if he got angry, he would think nothing of pulling a gun on someone.

Tara, it got so bad that for awhile I would blow up in anger at nothing. Absolutely nothing. I would find myself grinding my teeth at night and crying all the time. At one point, I even considered ending it all. Actually my husband and I both did.

Finally, I couldn't do it anymore. I couldn't carry it myself. And I knew I had to surrender my son to God. And it wasn't an instantaneously process. I had to surrender him over and over again.

And especially as a mother, that is so terribly hard to do, because we want to be able to fix it for them. But we can't.
No. And it was especially hard because some of our church family judged us and told us that if we were better parents, he wouldn't be that way.

Oh, that is so heartbreaking.

What's interesting is, when I finally surrendered, when I finally gave it to God and admitted that there was nothing else I could do, I was finally able to share with others. Not hide so much. And looking back, I can finally see the purpose for all of that. My son has had me counsel and help so many other mothers going through the exact same thing with their children.

I've finally realized that happiness is not joy. Was I happy through that terrible time? No, but I finally had a peace and a joy in Christ. He served five years in prison and in the last year he was saved.

So, from what you described early, it seems pretty apparent that both you and your husband went through a fairly significant battle with depression.
Yes.

Was it different for each of you?

Well, we both wanted to end it but my husband was more ready to actually end his life. But honestly, I never had that desire. I just wanted to run away. To form a new identity, a new life somewhere else. A way to salvage and rebuild and hide my shame.

What hurts is that even now, years later, some people at our church still want nothing to do with my son. He has never once preached at our church.

Really? Oh, that is sad. So much for being a new creature in Christ, huh?
(laughs) Apparently Jesus' blood can cover everything *except* for his past sins, I guess. He came once to our church to share his testimony and a couple of people got up and left.

It was really interesting that after he shared his story and what God had done, a friend of ours came up to me and looked so sad. He said, "Kathy, all those years you asked us to pray over and over for him. I'm ashamed to say that I wouldn't pray for him, because he was hopeless. But now I am so, so sorry."

Wow. How sad for him and how heartbreaking for you to hear.

It was sad, but thank God, He is doing great things through my son's ministry. And like I said, I realize now what the purpose was for going through all that. I've been able to help so many others.

~ ~ ~

As you can see, the causes and trials of depression are broad and multi-faceted; and we have barely scratched the surface here.

If you glean nothing else from this read, please remember this: depression does not determine your spiritual wellness.

I have a friend who I love dearly. He recently stated, "I think if a person is depressed, it's just because their heart is not right with the Lord." Really?

Depression is one of those things that is easy to judge unless you've lived it. Especially in cases of abuse or a simple chemical imbalance. My friend's comment was like saying, "If a person has diabetes, it's because their heart isn't right with the Lord."

Sometimes there is something that needs to be examined: an unaddressed sin problem or the like. However, that is the exception...not the rule. As we mentioned earlier, if Christians never got depressed, we wouldn't have most of the psalms. Poor David was depressed most of his life, bless his heart. And sometimes, depression can be a satanic attack after a great spiritual victory. Check out Elijah's moody blues after the battle at Mt. Carmel in I Kings 18.

But no matter the cause, or the form it takes, it can be fought and overcome.

My dear friend Kathy Vernich recently sent me her thoughts. After suffering years of abuse and suicidal depression, she is finding hope once again:

> *When the weight of your problems become heavy*
> *And seem too much to bear*
> *You feel that nobody is on your side*
> *One more thing could break the levy*
> *There comes a point that you don't care*
> *All you want to do is hide*
> *...To make a change will take time*
> *Learning to look at the positive*
> *It cannot turn on a dime*
> *Remember God chose you to live*

This remarkably brave woman was molested as a young person, as well as being introduced to pornography. After her husband left her with a five week old baby at the age of twenty one, Kathy became extremely depressed.

"Sometime in 2005, I got to the point that I didn't care about anything. That was when I first got on meds for depression. I wasn't completely honest with my doctor on the extent of my depression so the meds helped some but I was still down. I kept having thoughts of hitting a tree in my car so it would look like an accident. On May 4, 2006, God let that happen. I was driving in heavy rainfall when my car started to spin. It all went very slow. I did hit trees but it clipped my trunk...A quarter spin farther would have been my door. The driver's seat broke; I blacked out for a second....I know God had His hand on me and my car. There were no other cars involved; the impact was on the trunk causing my car to stop just a few feet from a swollen creek. Two days later outside of my house, I walked around looking at my car. I squatted down and started crying. I called a friend, couldn't talk...only cry...."

Several years later, and after life throwing her some pretty hard curve balls, Kathy told her friend what she was struggling with after a Wednesday evening church service. Little did her friend know that she'd been contemplating suicide.

"We had a long talk and I told her all about the night before. She hugged me as I shook and told her that I was scared. I gave her the clips to my pistol...My church family watches me. There are two friends that have all access to talk to my psychiatrist. There is no way to hide things now. Those two can read me very well; they can even tell if I'm down through a text message. If there are a few days that they don't see me or hear from me, they contact me to check and see how I'm doing... I'm doing better but I still have bad days. I think I've finally accepted that I will be on meds long term; maybe even for the rest of my life. It's a slow process but I'm making progress! God has put some amazing Christians in my life. I know I would not be here if it wasn't for Him!"

See what I mean when I say we should be the hands and feet of Jesus? Without the support of loving friends, Kathy's story might have had a much different ending.

I pray you've learned much from studying landmine number two: depression. Before we leave, I feel I'd be remiss if we didn't spend a few minutes talking about depression landmines for more than the average joe. Let's take a look at pastors who are struck by the explosion of depression.

You know, pastors can feel like victory is hollow too. And that is what section five is all about.

Hollow Victory · 111

Depression Section 5: A Special Look at Pastors and Depression

"Considering the way the world is, how broken and messy and considering how much the enemy likes to attack God's people, I think, 'Shouldn't we ALL be depressed?'"

~*April Colliers*

It's taboo. A major no-no. Pastors *never* deal with stuff like depression. They certainly are never suicidal…..right?

Um, no. Talk of depression among pastors is often pushed under the rug. Oftentimes, by the pastors themselves.

Thom S. Rainer declares, "Depression was once a topic reserved for 'other people'. It certainly was not something those in vocational ministry experienced. Perhaps it would be more accurate to say that ministers rarely admitted that they were depressed. After all, weren't these servants of God supposed to have their acts together? How could pastors and other ministers who have the call of God on their lives experience the dark valley of depression?"

I'm a PK (aka-preacher's kid for all those non PKs out there). Being in pastor's family helps you see all aspects of ministry: the good, the bad and the ugly. Believe me when I say that depression is a very real issue among pastors today.

According to *Lifeline for Pastors* (a publication from Maranatha Life):

- 1,500 pastors leave the ministry each month due to moral failure, spiritual burnout or contention in their churches.
- 80% of pastors and 84% of their spouses feel unqualified and discouraged in their role as pastors.
- 85% of pastors said their greatest problem is they are sick and tired of dealing with problem people, such as disgruntled elders, deacons, worship leaders, worship teams, board members, and associate pastors. 90% said the hardest thing about ministry is dealing with uncooperative people.
- 90% said the ministry was completely different than what they thought it would be before they entered the ministry.

To be honest, I've had a hard time finding people willing to talk with me about this. Most pastors I approached about this topic admit they have struggled with it but when asked if I could interview them, they said "No! If my congregation knew, I would lose all my credibility!" The stigma especially seems strong if the pastor is taking medication for his depression.

Many feel shame for their depression, and reticence to share with anyone tends to make the problem worse. "Clergy do not talk about it because it violates their understanding of their faith," says Steve Scoggin, president of CareNet, a network of 21 pastoral counseling centers in North Carolina . "They believe they are not supposed to have those kinds of thoughts." (Greg Warner, USA Today)

Dealing with mental illness is tough enough, but Christians can make it worse by "over-spiritualizing" depression.

Believers uneducated in understanding mental illness dismiss this issue as a lack of faith or a sign of weakness.

So rather than have their faith questioned, many pastors suffer silently. Avoidance becomes the goal. It is a high profile, high-stress job with nearly impossible expectations for success.

A Wounded Shepherd

Pastors are often called 'shepherds'...the overseers who lead their church flock. The question is then, what is wounding these shepherds so deeply?

1. **Spiritual warfare.** "The enemy does not want God's servants to be effective in ministry. He will do whatever it takes to hurt ministers and their ministries." (Thom S. Rainer)

2. **Exhaustion.** "A pastor is like a 24-hour ER who is supposed to be available to any congregant at any time...we create an environment that makes it hard to admit our humanity." (Steve Scoggin, Warner) Workaholism leads to burnout. Burnout leads to depression.

3. **Unrealistic expectations..** Pastors are expected to be at everyone's beck and call, deliver ground-breaking sermons each week, visit the sick, have perfect children, be hospitable, counsel the hurting and lead the entire church body through teaching and example. These expectations are enormous and unrealistic. "We set the bar so high that most pastors can't achieve that," said H.B. London, vice president for pastoral ministries at Focus on the Family. "And because most pastors are people-pleasers, they get frustrated and feel they can't live up to that."

And let's face it: pastors are dealing in weighty stuff. When you consider that their work impacts eternity...well, the pressure can be crushing. Sometimes the demands don't only come externally; they are often self-imposed. So when they think they are failing, they can turn their frustration back on themselves. A sure recipe for hopelessness.

4. **Criticism**. There is a wide-spread fable that ministry is a romantic line of service. You know...kneeling down in the streets of Calcutta, offering water to an orphan who later grows up to declare that due to *your* devotion and God's love, they will now spread the gospel in Africa.

Let me stop right here and say *ministry is not always warm fuzzies and sweet memories*. Honestly, ministry is all about serving others...others who happen to be sinners. There are a lot of crazies out there doing things 'in Jesus' name'. I'm convinced that if people knew half of what went on behind the scenes in a church, they would be shocked.

People can be critical. Harsh. Opinionated. And sometimes, down-right mean. And the pastor often gets the brunt of the criticism. In addition, in our modern world there is even more exposure. Facebook, twitter, podcasts, youtube...which all have great potential to spread the Gospel, but also create even more opportunities for a pastor to take a hit.

5. **Family problems.** The average pastor is often torn between his never-ending duties and spending time with his family. If he's not careful, the wife and kids will feel neglected. Then add in financial stress. Ministers are often underpaid and take a bullet on their taxes as well, since they are taxed as 'self-employed'. The church family's needs will sometimes creep in and affect the harmony of the home. And the pastor's wife is supposed to be okay with sharing her husband. My mother is a pastor's wife and jokingly quips that someday she will write a book about being a minister's wife. She plans to title it *Others May But You May Not*.

Growing up as PK, there were a lot of interesting things that would happen in the church that affected our home life. It seemed like every time my family would plan a family vacation, somebody in the church would die. I remember feeling terrible if we planned a family vacation because I felt sure that it would doom some poor, unsuspecting church member to meet the Lord early.

You may wonder why I picked the title *A Wounded Shepherd*. Pastors are supposed to lead, protect and love God's lambs.

But oftentimes, the picture is more accurate of a shepherd fallen on the ground, while a wolf attacks him over and over. The sheep stand nearby, calming chewing on their cud. As he fights for his life, one of the sheep leans over to the other and says, "You know, he could be doing much better at taking care of us. And honestly, I don't think he's done an adequate job feeding me lately..."

Meanwhile, the shepherd is exhausted and bleeding, begging for relief.

Elijah

This really isn't a new phenomenon. It's been going on since Bible times. Consider Elijah.

In I Kings 19, Elijah had just defeated the false prophets of Baal. This was a huge spiritual victory! And all done in a very grandiose, public fashion. He should have been on cloud nine.

Yet, one discouraging message and threat from the evil queen Jezebel, and Elijah panicked and ran.

> *"He himself went a day's journey into the desert. He came to a broom tree, sat down under it and prayed that he might die. 'I have had enough, LORD,' he said. 'Take my life; I am no better than my ancestors.' Then he lay down under the tree and fell asleep...."* (verses 4-5)

Elijah had insisted that his servant leave him. He was isolated and alone. Refusing the encouragement of fellow believers, especially when we're already down, is a prime time to begin listening to those negative thoughts. When all we have is our own depressed viewpoint, the company isn't good.

> *"All at once an angel touched him and said, 'Get up and eat.' He looked around, and there by his head was a cake of bread baked over hot coals, and a jar of water. He ate and drank and then lay down again.*
> *The angel of the LORD came back a second time and touched him and said, 'Get up and eat, for the journey is too much for you.' So he got up and ate and drank." (verses 5-8)*

Such a beautiful picture of God's care. The Almighty sent an angel to care for Elijah's physical needs. God is concerned about every aspect of our lives. And depression very much involves giving attention to our physical bodies, as well as our emotional and spiritual body.

It's easy to forget that God doesn't just care about our spiritual state: He cares about each and every part of us. He wants us to be whole, complete and happy in Him. Did you notice that in this passage, God took care of all three of Elijah's needs? He gave him food, water and rest for his physical body, comforted him emotionally and then addressed the spiritual issue that had caused Elijah to run in fear. God is the ultimate holistic healer!

The passage goes on to say that God Himself came to comfort Elijah and remind him that he was not alone in his struggle.

Shining a Light in the Darkness

There is one pastor who, when I asked for an interview, readily and happily agreed. His joy is contagious and his courage is unparalleled. I'd like you to meet my friend Steve...

When did your depression begin?

In 1994, I was visiting at a hospital in Little Rock. When I came out, it was starting to get dark. In the parking garage I was jumped by two guys. They beat me up pretty badly. They didn't get anything from me but my pride.

They tried to sexually assault me and rob me. Before they could, someone drove by. It scared them and they took off.

That's horrible!
The stigma was awful. I reported the attack to the police and they made fun of me. "A big guy like you couldn't fend those guys off?..." I was so upset that I left.

That attack started all of it. I started having headaches, nightmares of the assault, cold sweats...I eventually fell into a depression.

How did you deal with it?

Well, I was pastoring and working a full time job. I was having to deal with my own stuff as well as the church's stuff. The depression tail-spinned for about six years.

I couldn't seem to shake it. I had so many flashbacks of the attack. During that time, I slept about three to four hours a night. At a pastor's associational meeting, I ended up talking to a pastor friend's wife. The story came out and she shared how she had been attacked in the past as well. I drew a lot of strength from her.

I finally told my wife.

Wait---you didn't tell your wife when it happened?

No, I hid it from her. And it was extra hard because I'm a former alcoholic---all I wanted was a drink.

In 2003, a tornado hit McCrory, Arkansas and damaged our church. That stress brought on another tailspin. At that time I starting having major anxiety. Keep in mind, I was teaching at the seminary in Oxford, Mississippi and pastoring...still, I couldn't sleep.

I resigned my church and moved to another church and was there for about three years. A false accusation was made against me. Church members were calling me at home and threatening me.

Wow! That's some major, devastating stress.

One day, I became overwhelmed and pulled out my gun. I remember grabbing my pistol in one hand while my bullets were in the other. I thought about how easy it would be to end it.

Staring at that pistol in my fingers, I finally came to myself. "There's no sense in this," I thought. I put my gun and bullets away and called the VA suicide hotline. I saw the psychologist that morning. I told him I was suffering from anxiety, panic and flashbacks.

In the midst of all this, I had prostate cancer and back surgery. I was beside myself. It was normal for my blood pressure to shoot up and then plummet. Frankly, I was a physical and spiritual mess.

The psychologist told me I had a classic symptoms of trauma and anxiety. He advised me to avoid any pressure or stress for three months. I asked "How can I do that? I'm a pastor!" *(laughs)*

I've been in treatment for panic and anxiety for about two years now. The great thing is now I know God is for me and I can understand what others are going through. In a crowd, I can just look and pick out the folks who are suffering like I used to be.

Comforting others the way you were comforted.

Yes! And I've discovered my family has a history of alcoholism and depression. I didn't know about it because it was never talked about. When I share my story, people seemed shocked that I know how they feel. But I've been there.

God got me through my problems. And He's the key. God has given me a purpose- not just to preach, but to share myself — it helps others — and it helps me in the process.

If you could go back in time and change that day you were attacked in that parking lot---if you could erase it to keep it from happening, would you?

No, I wouldn't change that attack. It's helped me rely on God.

What advice would you pass along to others?

My advice is: get help. Go to a therapist. It's not gonna magically disappear. You can't do it on your own. Find a preacher that's been through it. And medication will probably be needed. Accept it. And remember that God will help you. He can handle it.

For the Church Member Lending a Hand... or Two

- *Pray for your pastor.* The best way to ward off satanic attack is to cover him and his family with prayer.

- ***Encourage vacations.*** "Make certain your pastor takes time off every year. Vacations must be mandatory. He likewise needs to take at least one day off each week. Look for signs that he is not giving sufficient time to his family, and help him to find the time to do so. His wife and children cannot be neglected." (Thom S. Ranier)
- ***Financial.*** Work as a church to make sure your pastor is being given adequate compensation. *"...the worker deserves his wages." (Luke 10:7) NIV*
  - Some churches won't allow the pastors to work second jobs, but also can't afford to pay him near what his family needs to survive. So his wife ends up having to work one, or sometimes, even two jobs. My pastor friend Bill Driggers stated, "That happens a lot and it's so hard on the family. You have to be willing to pay the pastor what his family needs to stay afloat or at least allow him to work. It creates a lot of resentment on the wife's part too if she has to do all the bread winning and her husband is always gone taking care of everybody else."
  - Remember, if *you* can't live on it, your pastor can't either.

- ***Don't be a time hog.*** Driggers says, "Be respectful of your pastor's time. He needs his study time. You know, just respect those boundaries. And of course, the world is so different now. Pastors today never get a break at all because of this," he declares, as he pats the cell phone case on his hip. "This has totally changed everything about ministry. I cannot tell you how many times a day our senior pastor gets called. It's absolutely nonstop. You know, call on your pastor for the emergencies but don't call him to tell him how

your runny nose is doing. A good rule of thumb is call on the Lord more than you call your pastor."
- **Encouragement and gifts.** Encourage your pastor to share at other churches when he has the opportunity to preach in other venues. It will do his heart a world of good to minister to fresh faces now and then.
  - And who doesn't love an encouraging card from time to time? Verbally encourage him, slip a gift into his office at random times (Not just on Pastor Appreciation Day). Listen to him if he needs to talk. Organize a 'food pounding' from the church: a special time set aside to give his family dry goods, gift cards, etc. Those special moments of 'loving' on your pastor will make a world of difference in his work.

For the Pastor...

- *Take time to relax.* Even Jesus took time alone to pray and recharge His battery. Sometimes for an extended period of time.
- **Make your family a priority.** Your family is a ministry too. Don't be afraid to think long term about how your children will grow up to view God's work and ministry. "One thing I always tried to do was make my kids part of the 'rewards' part of ministry," Driggers added. "If a church gave me a $200 Christmas bonus, we would give a good chunk of that to our kids and tell them, 'We know it's hard in ministry sometimes, but there are also spiritual and physical benefits too. I'd like to share my bonus with you, because you are such a huge support to me.' I think it's important for pastors to help their children recognize the advantages and blessings of working in ministry; not just griping about the hard stuff."

- **Set boundaries.** I think of Moses; how did he manage to lead and pastor over a million people without cracking? And you know, those Israelites did some complaining! "We're hungry...we're thirsty...we want meat...we're sick of meat...we're tired of manna...it was better in slavery...Moses, are you trying to kill us?" His father-in-law Jethro even noticed how badly the people were draining Moses. He encouraged him to set boundaries and delegate responsibility. Moses heeded Jethro's wisdom and saved himself from years of mental and physical anguish.
- **Find a confidante.** Ask God to send you a friend, a fellow pastor or confidante that you can share openly with; someone who will listen, point you up to Christ, pray with you and can keep a confidence.
- **Seek medical help if the depression persists.** Contrary to popular belief, needing medication does not mean you're crazy. It means your human with a mortal body that wears out from time to time. Medication is simply a tool God has provided to help until we receive those glorified bodies He's promised us.
- **Nurture your relationship with God.** You can't give what you don't have. You will have a hard time dropping love and truth into the church folks if you are dry and empty.

When asked what advice he would give to young pastors, Bill Driggers offered this wisdom: "If you want to stay in it for the long haul, you have to maintain your closeness to the Lord. Everybody is going to be pulling on you from every direction and you *have* stay close to Him if you want to make it. And being a pastor is more than just studying; it's about serving people and loving them."

Recovery from the landmine of depression is possible. Hope abounds. Reach for it. Reach for Christ and the rest He can give.

The Wound

So whether you're a shepherd or a sheep, we've discussed lots of great stuff on how to identify and deal with depression. Remember to consider that this landmine can continue to explode in your life if your depression is indeed driven by your core wound.

Consider the list of possible causes. Ask God to help reveal the source of your wound to you if it's His will. This will be the first step towards healing and freedom from the landmine of depression. Ask Him to help you disarm it. And then do the work it requires. Be proactive. I love the old saying, "Don't ask the Lord to guide your footsteps if you are not willing to move your feet."

Be sure to check out the Study Guide for even more help, as well as a sample Victory Journal on pages 17-20.

Identifying your hidden wound is one of the toughest parts of the recovery process. Be patient with yourself but don't stop searching. And hey, if you need ongoing help to identify your needs and wounds, feel free to contact me at:

Tara@TaraJohnsonMinistries.com
Twitter @TaraMinistry
www.TaraJohnsonMinistries.com

Encouraging each other is what it's all about and I'm here to assist you in whatever way I can. My ministry is full of tools prepared to help. I've been right where you are!

God wants to heal you. He wants you living in joy, freedom and the beautiful hope He's offered.

I leave you with this thought from Betsy Ten Boom:

"There is no pit so deep that
God's love is not deeper still."

LANDMINE #3 : PERFECTIONISM

"Perfectionism will not only rob you of your freedom, it will make you a horrible bore."

~Steve Brown

Ah, perfectionism. It doesn't look like a landmine. It doesn't feel like a landmine. But that's the point. It's deceptively dangerous. This particular trap is likely to set off other explosions around you. Want to know what I mean? Let's tiptoe around it and see...

Shattering the Fairytale

The Disney princesses messed me up.

I confess I had quite a fascination with them when I was growing up (After I finished my Princess Leia phase, that is). I *was* going to be as beautiful as Aurora and I *was* going to have a grand adventure like Belle. And I *was* going to be a singer like Ariel. Or at the very least, a marine biologist...

But let's get real for a moment, shall we?

There was one big problem with all those Disney beauties...they had no flaws.

Don't get me wrong. What made them such great heroines was their resilience in adversity. But they weren't real. They lived a dreamy haze of melody filled daydreams that somehow managed to blossom into perfect endings. No residual anger. No emotional baggage. At least none that we ever hear about.

Aurora (aka Sleeping Beauty) should have had abandonment issues, not to mention a prescription for narcolepsy. Cinderella was emotionally and physically abused, yet never struggled with anger or fear.

Belle married a guy with a bad temper and mood swings. Think they might have had marital trouble down the road? Rapunzel was kidnapped, married a convicted criminal and should have been socially backwards. Snow White had that shrill voice and Ariel changed into a whole other species. Talk about confusion!

Steven Sondheim had some valuable insight in his hit Broadway musical *Into the Woods*.
In this story, all of the great fairytale characters' lives intersect: Jack and the Beanstalk, Cinderella, Red Riding Hood, the baker and his wife, Rapunzel...and the first act is what you would imagine. Beautiful arias full of hope and a longing to find their true love. And they all find their happily ever after.

But the second act of *Into the Woods* tells a much different story. Cinderella and her prince are bored with each other. Rapunzel has uncontrollable depression from her past abuse and drives her husband crazy with her nonstop weeping fits. Red Riding Hood had such fun killing the wolf that she becomes a blood thirsty hunter. You get the idea.

And the conclusion of the musical is this: be careful what you wish for. Sometimes what we long for is truly not the best for us.

See, I have finally realized that those Disney princesses with their perfect figures, perfect hair, perfect dramas, perfect princes and perfect endings made me think that, well, that I could perfect too.

And I'm not.

I know, I know. You're shocked. But do you know how many hours I've spent trying to live in 'happily ever after'?

I'm a perfectionist. I want my house to be clean...not just picked up but CLEAN. I want to be a size 6. I want to be a beacon of spirituality that lights the path for others. And I want my neighborhood to be like Mayberry.

Can you relate to this? If I'm not mistaken, this mentality and way of life is called *perfectionism*.

Thankfully, I can say that I am no longer a full blown perfectionist, but rather a recovering perfectionist. And if you are wondering, 'recovering' simply means that at least I'm aware of it now and am *trying* to chill.

Other than being brain washed by the Disney princesses, there are many different reasons for perfectionism:

A Need For Control

Now don't get testy with me here. This isn't really as bad as it sounds. This doesn't mean that you run around bossing others with a scolding finger in their face. It might mean that you are a natural leader or that circumstances beyond your control affected you deeply when you were younger. So in turn, you have a need to control simply to maintain a feeling of security and normalcy. In many young girls with eating disorders, researchers have found that they refuse to eat simply because that is the one thing in their life that they *can* control.

Control provides the illusion of:

- A sense of certainty
- Completion of items on our 'to do' list, so we don't have to worry about them
- Being able to predict what will happen
- That people (including ourselves) and things are consistent to achieve perfect peace in a messy world

Let me stop here and remind you that it provides the *illusion* of certainty and security but that is often not reality.

I relate to this. I don't like spontaneity. It makes my stomach cramp. If I can schedule a time to be spontaneous, then I'm good. Having a change in my plans threatens my feelings of security and well-being. Life suddenly becomes scary and unsafe when I have too many surprises in a day.

The Need For Approval

If you are a perfectionist, you may have learned early in life that other people valued you because of how much you accomplished or achieved. As a result, you may have learned to value yourself only on the basis of other people's approval.

So you may think that your value comes to be based primarily on external standards. This can leave you vulnerable and overly sensitive to the opinions and criticism of others. I know this is very true for myself! The only way that I can protect myself from criticism is to never fail. And that is a very heavy load to carry.

Genetically Predisposed

You ever hear of a 'type A' personality? Yep, that's a ranting and raving perfectionist. Sometimes it's a learned behavior, but often times the drive for perfection is often passed down from generation to generation.

Some people are just more competitive than others, more sensitive than others, etc. God makes us all different with unique talents and abilities. If He has given you a drive to strive for excellence, that is a very good thing! The trouble comes when we get out of balance and begin to obsess about being perfect instead of just striving for excellence.

Fear Of Failure And Making Mistakes

For some reason, in my mind, mistakes often equal failure. And that is not true! Mistakes provide us with opportunities to learn, to grow, to be creative. And failing to achieve a goal does not mean that I don't have value. It just means I'm human.

Many perfectionists have, what I call, black and white syndrome. It's a view point of extremes...either all or none. A straight "A" student who receives a "B" might believe, "I'm a total failure."

In addition, our lives are consumed with 'shoulds'. I *should* read my Bible. I *should* go to church. I *should* love that person that is driving me crazy. The problem with 'shoulds' is that they stress obedience without proper motivation. In Arkansas terms, it means your heart ain't right!

Fear Of Disapproval

For many perfectionists, disapproval equals loss of love. So they will try their hardest to hide their flaws to keep being accepted as well as working their hardest to keep everyone around them happy. Often times, perfectionism and the landmine of people-pleasing go hand in hand.

The Washing Machine

Perfectionists live in a vicious cycle. First they set lofty goals that are incredibly hard to reach. The constant pressure to perform leads to anxiety and reduces their ability to work effectively. Then they fail to reach those goals because they were unrealistic to begin with. Then the self criticism and guilt begin to chip away at their mental and emotional state until they are knee deep in inner turmoil. Yet, they think "maybe if I try harder, I will succeed" which sets the whole washing machine spinning again.

Then Tuesday begins.

The real tragedy of perfectionism is in the unintended results: anxiety and depression for starters. And without even realizing it, perfectionists may unintentionally apply their high standards on to others, becoming critical, demanding or resentful. They usually try to avoid letting anyone see their mistakes, not realizing that honesty and the ability 'to be real' are attractive qualities to others. They hide who they truly are and oftentimes suffer from strained and distant personal relationships.

I love the way a friend of mine put it:

"I think the core center of my perfectionism comes from being judged. I have always felt very judged. I get depressed because I have these lofty goals and when I don't meet them, I give up. When you give up, people judge and can be hard on you. It's a bad cycle. So basically I have learned not to judge others.(laughs) Probably another lofty goal I'll never reach!"

So here's the thing...

In my own opinion, getting down to the heart of the matter is this: we all crave unconditional love.

Remember how we talked about 'the hole inside' during the introduction? We have a cavern where we used to have a complete and perfect connection with God. But when we messed up, that connection was severed. And we've been trying to fill it ever since.

In *Searching for God Knows What*, Donald Miller shares how he has come to understand this need inside of us. He says he imagines what it would be like if an alien came to our planet and observed us. He would see us watching our competitive reality shows and ball games and wonder what's wrong with us.

" 'You guys', the alien might say, 'you are obsessed. You have to wear a certain kind of clothes, drive a certain car, speak a certain way, live in a certain neighborhood, whatever, all of it so you can be higher on an invisible hierarchy. It's an obsession!...It is as though something that helped them function and live well has gone missing, and they are pining for that missing thing in all sorts of odd methods, none of which are working.' "

We all try to fill that hole with something: food, relationships, sex, drugs, alcohol, money, power...and yes, even approval and control.

Those Disney princesses tried to fill that hole too, with their ideal of the perfect prince who would give them a perfect future and a perfect, unselfish love. But the only One who can give us all those things is Jesus Christ. Yet, we all continue to look for unconditional love in conditional people. A sure way to make victorious living feel hollow and unsatisfying.

And let me tell you through experience, perfectionism is a moving target. It can't be done. And trying to make it work will trigger the landmine to explode.

So what are we going to do about it?

Get Your Shovel Ready

We are going to dig a little deeper here.

> *"Not that I have already obtained all this, or have already arrived at my goal, but I press on to take hold of that for which Christ Jesus took hold of me. Brothers and sisters, I do not consider myself yet to have taken hold of it. But one thing I do: Forgetting what is behind and straining toward what is ahead, I press on toward the goal to win the prize for which God has called me heavenward in Christ Jesus." ~Philippians 3:12-14*

Again, Paul reminds us that the goal is 'excellence' and 'determination'; not perfection.

Remind yourself that God loves you no matter how well, or how poorly you perform

> *"In all these things we are more than conquerors through him who loved us. For I am convinced that neither death nor life, neither angels nor demons, neither the present nor the future, nor any powers, neither height nor depth, nor anything else in all creation, will be able to separate us from the love of God that is in Christ Jesus our Lord."*
> Romans 8:37-39

You did nothing to earn His love and there is nothing you can do to lose it. At the end of your life, you will not stand before your peers...you'll stand before Him. Pleasing Him is all that matters.

Surround yourself with safe people

Safe people are those who love you whether you have it together or not. They encourage you to draw closer to God. They speak the truth in love and show mercy and forgiveness. They give us strength in setting boundaries and fuel your soul with encouragement. Run hard and fast from manipulators. If you do everything well, there are those who will take advantage of you.

Forgive yourself when you mess up

I know that majorly messing up is a death sentence for a perfectionist. I get it. But that doesn't change the fact that you *will* mess up. Accept it.

You're not God, which by default means that you're an imperfect creature who will let someone down at some point. When it happens, confess it to the Lord and move on.

Schedule times to be 'unperfect'

Boy, I know this is hard but do it anyways. Go grocery shopping with no make up on. Wear grungy clothes on an errand. Trying painting a picture and making it as ugly as possible. I know it sounds crazy but you might be surprised at the freedom you will discover. Find a place that you can go to totally and completely relax. No performing; just a place where you can be yourself with the Lord. That might be at a special spot in your house, on a nature walk, or in the car, for instance.

Confess your feelings to God

Confess it. Tell Him all of it. Don't hold back. The amazing thing about our Savior is that He knows it all anyways. He listens as we cry, rejoice and pour out our frustrations. He is your safe haven and longs to help you walk in complete freedom.

Try to unearth the source of your perfectionism

This takes courage. Ask yourself about your motives. Why do you do what you do?

And then after you have figured that out, dig deeper.

I'll show you what I mean. Not too long ago, I was reading *Inside Out* by Larry Crabb which God used to teach me a lot about my own motives. I have a few close friends but while being very friendly, I tend to hold people at a distance.

Sometimes when the phone rings, even not knowing who is on the other end, I want to run. So I asked myself why. Here is how the internal conversation went:

Well, I want to run because it might be someone who will want me 'to do' something for them.

Would that be so bad?

Not necessarily. But I've had bad experiences with needy people. In the past, they have taken advantage of me. They don't respect my boundaries and that sucks my energy dry.

Why do you think that is?

I just told you why! I'm a people pleaser!

Dig deeper. What if it isn't someone wanting you to give you a 'to do' list? What if it is just someone wanting to chat?

I still want to run away from that ringing phone.

Why? Dig deeper.

Close friendships scare me.

Why?

Because if they get close to me, they might see how broken I really am inside. They will think less of me. They won't love me anymore.

See what I mean?

I believe that if we are fearless enough to be honest, to search our hearts and ask God to shine His light on our brokenness, He will reveal ground-breaking and life-changing awareness to our minds and spirits. And He can transform us to be people who live in freedom, no longer chained to the cycle of perfectionism and anxiety.

The Conclusion Of The Matter

Alright, so I didn't grow up to be as pretty as Aurora or visit an enchanted castle like Belle, but my imperfect life is actually a pretty neat adventure with Christ. And I'm tasting true freedom for the first time.

And I can claim that someday my Prince *will* come. He will split the sky and ride in on His white horse, transforming this broken, messy world and will take me home to be with Him forever.

And I will place a crown at His feet and forever sing His praises along with all the redeemed and every creature in Heaven. "And so shall we ever be with the Lord."

Now *that* will be a perfectly happily ever after...

Hollow Victory · 137

Perfectionism Section 2: How God Sees Us

So the big question is, regardless of how we view our efforts, how does God see them?

I think that much of the problem with perfectionism comes in when we actually begin comparing ourselves to others instead of our Creator. We think, "Well, compared to so-and-so, I'm doing great! I've got it going on."
Bad idea.

My two little dogs are bichons. They are adorable little critters with fluffy white fur and big brown eyes. I love their white coats and even use whitening shampoo during their baths. They stand up next a golden retriever or a black lab and they look beautifully pristine.

Last winter, we had a snowfall and our family gathered around to watch them play in the drifts. I was shocked! They looked dingy and yellow. Compared to other dogs they looked perfect, but standing in a fresh, pure snowfall, they looked filthy. Disgusting, actually.

Let's face it, the people in the New Testament who were the most glaringly obvious perfectionists were the Pharisees. I know...drawing a comparison between that self-righteous bunch and myself stings a little. But self-reflection usually does that very thing. Be brave, my friend! Keep peering intently into the mirror. The results could be life-changing. Looking in could be the difference in a happy life or a broken one.

In Luke 16, Jesus had just gotten through teaching that a person cannot serve two masters. The Pharisees were no fans of Jesus. They had tried to bubble themselves inside the protection of the Law, self-deception and works. But Jesus punched too many holes in their perfect balloons.

The Pharisees were sneering at Jesus as He taught. "And he said to them, 'You are those who justify yourselves before men, but God knows your hearts. For what is exalted among men is an abomination in the sight of God.'" (Luke 16:15 ESV)

You see, our standard is not in each other. Our standard is Christ. That's a hard pill for a perfectionist to swallow. *"All of us have become like one who is unclean, and all our righteous acts are like filthy rags..."* (Isaiah 64:6 NIV)

But don't be disheartened! If you have claimed Jesus as your Savior, God no longer sees your filthiness; He sees the beauty of His Son stamped on your heart.

Read Romans 8:1-4 and be encouraged!

> *There is therefore now no condemnation for those who are in Christ Jesus. For the law of the Spirit of life has set you free in Christ Jesus from the law of sin and death. For God has done what the law, weakened by the flesh, could not do. By sending his own Son in the likeness of sinful flesh and for sin, he condemned sin in the flesh, in order that the righteous requirement of the law might be fulfilled in us... (ESV)*

So should we strive for excellence? Absolutely! *"So whether you eat or drink or whatever you do, do it all for the glory of God."* (I Corinthians 10:31 NIV) But perfection? No, because that has already been achieved by Christ.

The key is balance. And a sure way to find that balance is to check your motives. Next time you're striving to be the perfect teacher, make the best cookies, whatever it is, ask yourself, "Am I doing this so others will think better of me or is it because I'm trying to give my best to God?" If you're honest, I think the majority of the time, the motive is to catch the attention of those around us. Those 'atta-boys' feel pretty good to our flesh.

But what about those of you who are thinking, "Wait! God said 'Be ye perfect as I am perfect'"? Oftentimes, the original language that states 'perfect', actually means 'whole or complete'.

If you look up definitions of 'whole', you find this: Containing all components...not divided...restored...healed...a thing lacking no part.

This makes a big difference doesn't it? It doesn't mean that we are not flawed but that we should strive to be complete in Christ. Seeking wisdom, strength, showing fruits of the spirit, loving one another, growing in Him...you get the idea.

Bed-making

God's view of our efforts is best summed up by my hairstylist April. She says, "You know, it's kind of like me watching my little girl make her bed. She tugs and pulls those sheets and covers; tries to arrange the pillows before proudly proclaiming, 'Look, Momma! I made my bed!' I walk in to her room and see the rumpled sheets and the lumps in the blanket but just smile at her effort. I never say, 'Are you nuts? This looks terrible!' She's only six. But I praise her and make a big deal out of it because she tried and gave it her all."

What a beautiful picture! If you have given your life to Christ, you are His princess. His prince. He delights in everything you do. Even when you color outside the lines, even when you have lumps in your blankets, even when you accidentally leave a smear of toothpaste behind on the counter, He loves you and His heart is thrilled to see you learning, trying and growing into a mature, complete person.

But don't take my word for it...

Here are some more thoughts from my inspiring friends...

Kathy

I love what you said about your closet. You told me that if I wanted proof that you weren't much of a perfectionist that I should just check out your closet. (*She laughs*) **I take it you haven't struggled much with perfectionism.**

Well, it depends. In some areas I demand much of myself or too much of others. Not my closet! (*laughs*) It's the things that I can't shut the door on that I want perfect. Those things I can't hide.

I love the way you put that. "The things I can't shut the door on…" What an interesting way to look at it.

Well, I've had to learn how to relax in some ways. I now have some foster kids in the house, ages two and three, so toys are everywhere. Every time I'm tempted to be frustrated by all the baby stuff and messes, I have to stop and remind myself 'Is it more important to look perfect or to invest in these kids?'

So I guess you weren't always as mellow as you have learned to be now. How did disorder and imperfection affect you when you were younger?

Oh, it drove me nuts. My mother kept everything. It was embarrassing and drove me crazy. And my husband is exactly like her! *(laughs)* I was the type that if there was any disorder, I would stay up all night cleaning, because if I didn't and someone came over, I would feel judged.

That is something that I've always struggled with. I want people to think the best of me and my children.

~ ~ ~

Evelyn

Have you ever struggled with perfectionism?

A little bit, but now I just strive for excellence instead of perfection. For me, I hate being unorganized, so when that happens, everything gets 'off' and my perspective begins to shift. Of course, for years I didn't realize the difference between excellence and perfection, but as we grow spiritually, we learn.

~ ~ ~

Marilyn

Have you ever struggled with perfectionism?

Yes, all of my life. My husband often says "You know, if you would just stop trying to make everything perfect, you could get a lot more done." *(laughs)* But I'd rather do it myself than see it done wrong. It's a hard thing because you want total control to see it done well so you take on all the responsibility yourself but you *know* that you need someone because it's overwhelming without it.

I remember one time we had a group in to our church to sing, one that my daughter was part of. Well, time came to get ready for them to come and we all knew that we needed to feed them but no one stepped up to offer. Since it was my idea to have them in, I volunteered to bring all the desserts and meat dishes myself. I ended up spending two or three days making 12 pies and bunches of other stuff. Looking back on that now, I think 'Why on earth did I do that?'

When you worked so hard during that time, what were your feelings about it?

Honestly, I don't even remember. I don't recall much from that time in my life. It's all a blur...I was so busy! I do remember not having a clue as to what was going on the in world, in the news because I was so busy trying to work and keep everything going perfectly. As I have gotten older, I have relaxed on that some. I don't care if my house isn't perfect anymore.

And honestly, that's why I gave up sewing. *(laughs)* If I can't do it perfectly, I'm not going to do it at all!

~ ~ ~

Christy

Have you ever struggled with perfectionism?

Yes, ma'am! I am a pk too...a missionary Baptist pk. I guess my daddy drilled it into my head that I didn't need to cause any interruptions in service. I sang a lot of specials but was so worried that if I messed up, it would end up ruining things before the sermon. I put so much pressure on myself.

I mean, like anxiety attacks and the whole bit.

When did those start?

About eight years ago. You know, the anxiety has been a gradual situation. And then I began to think, "This is just satan after me." But I couldn't shake it---so then I had guilt! I felt like satan was trying to cripple me.

Crystal

Yeah, I've struggled with perfectionism in the past. But one day it hit me that I was doing it for man, and not for God. It [Perfectionism] drove me, which is good, *but* when you cross the line into obsession, it's trouble!

~ ~ ~

Do you see how the strive for perfection can be a detrimental stumbling block in your journey? Again, excellence is the goal. But what does a life of excellence versus a life of perfectionism look like?

Well, I'm glad you asked. That's what we'll discuss in section three.

Perfectionism Section 3: Godly Imperfectionism in Action

So what does it look like to strive for excellence yet scrap the mantle of perfectionism? In my opinion, the hook that all of this hinges on is love.

> *"Therefore, be clear minded and self-controlled so that you can pray. Above all, love each other deeply. Because love covers a multitude of sins. ~I Peter 4:7,8*

When the motivation for everything we do is love, everything will change. We will want to do a good job but the strive for perfectionism (aka puffing up our pride) melts away.

The perfect example of what this looks like can be taken from a little town called Mayberry.

In *The Andy Griffith Show*, Mayberry's church was a very loving and accepting bunch of folks. One episode stands out in my mind as the epitome of what unconditional love will do.

Hollow Victory · 147

The Mayberry church choir is asked to compete in a singing competition. The townsfolk buzz with the excitement of the contest. To win would mean recognition and a little bit of limelight for the sleepy town.

Unfortunately, their star soloist becomes ill. The choir director is all aflutter trying to find a suitable replacement in such a short time. While complaining about the turn of events to Andy, Barney sees his moment of fame calling.

Barney tells the director that is a superb soloist...that he has even studied under a vocal coach. The choir director is suitably impressed and offers the solo to Barney on the spot.

But there's one problem: Barney can't sing.

Poor Barney is unaware of his, ahem, vocally challenged predicament. But it becomes glaringly obvious during the first rehearsal that allowing Barney to sing the solo and represent Mayberry would be a fiasco and huge embarrassment. What to do?

The choir tries meeting for rehearsals without him but he always manages to find out. Over time, his singing seems to get worse instead of better. Nobody wants to hurt his feelings, seeing what a sensitive a soul he is. So Sheriff Andy comes to the rescue.

On the day of the competition, Andy tells Barney that the mic he'll be using is a new top-of-the-line model. It's super sensitive and amplifies the tiniest sound. Andy encourages him to sing lower than a whisper or he will destroy everyone's hearing. Clueless Barney falls for this explanation. When it's time for his solo, their lead baritone sneaks into the back in front a pre-set up hot mic.

Barney timidly opened his mouth to sing and is amazed to hear the glorious, full body tone coming out of his mouth. He proudly puffs out his chest and performs his heart out, oblivious to the robust baritone singing over him. Everyone knew he couldn't sing but they very tactfully and lovingly created a situation where he would look good without damaging his fragile ego.

God intended His children to be a support system to each other. A huge danger with perfectionism is that as your ability to be 'perfect' increases, your tolerance for those who can't hit those standards decreases. In simple terms, you will unwittingly put more burdens on people than God intended them to bear. You unconsciously begin to demand that same perfectionism from those around you.

In other words, you can unintentionally set landmines for others to step on.

From Balance to Obsession

How can we know when we've teetered tottered on the wrong side of excellence and into obsessive perfection?
Well, here are a few warning signs:
- *Never satisfied with your performance*
- *Negative recurring and persistent thoughts.* These thoughts often cause anxiety and stress, as well as stating "Nothing you do is ever good enough."
- *A constant state of awareness of the lack of perfectionism in yourself or others.*
- *Refusing to deviate from guidelines or the way 'things are supposed to be'.*
- *Constantly fearing rejection.* This will take a good bit of awareness and self-reflection on your part.
- *When your mistakes feel like a death sentence.*
- *Refusing to change unhealthy behaviors because you might fail at the change.*
- *Thinking "I have no value in life unless I'm successful."*
- *Thinking that love = good performance*
- *Overt competitiveness.* "Unless I can be 'number one', I refuse to try."
- *Persistent low self-esteem*
- *Guilt over perceived failures*

- **Depression.** Not all depression is a result of perfectionism, but it can point to a deeper problem.
- ***Rigid, inflexible, non-spontaneous***
- **Obsessive-compulsive behavior.** Oftentimes, this indulgence is a way to make the perfectionist feel better about their mistakes. It places a superficial bandage on a deep wound.
- **Lack of motivation.** Fear of failure is reason to not try which causes immobility and stagnation. It's the never-ending sense of feeling 'stuck'.
- ***Eating disorders***
- ***General unhappiness and comparing yourself to others***

You see, none of the problems listed above are a result of loving God and others with abandon. It's the opposite. All these behaviors and thoughts are rooted in self-preservation, pride, feeling un-loved and the like.

Remember, if you have given your life to Jesus, You are redeemed. You are His. That means when God looks at you, He doesn't see your faults, your mess-ups or your train-wrecks. He sees the beauty and spotless essence of the Perfect Lamb. He doesn't expect us to be perfect; just faithful and loving to Him and each other. There is nothing you can do to earn His love and nothing you can do to take it away. He is love. Period.

Don't be confused here. God's love is unconditional. Perfect. When we grasp that concept, the freedom is completely staggering! But, people will still judge. It's part of our fallen, human nature. "Perfectionism is a moving target." So the sooner that you realize no matter what you do, some people will still view you as a failure, the more likely you'll be to accept this as a fact of life. Not a detriment to you or your value. People are just ornery and unloving sometimes.

Again, the measuring stick is not a comparison between you and your neighbor. You will not stand before your peers when this life is over. You'll be standing before your Savior. The One who loved you so much He died for you.

Loving The Imperfect

Several years back, our church went on a float trip down the Buffalo River in Arkansas. And I've got to say that though I am not a girly-girl, I like my makeup! I have very fair skin and when I try to go without makeup, people accuse me of having the flu. So people never see me without some sort of makeup on. Ever.

But on a four hour float trip down a river where the canoe keeps tipping, well, perfection is impossible. The whole church group was sunburned, tired and the women bore the mark of runny raccoon mascara eyes. The smart ones didn't even bother with mascara that day.

When we got back to camp, I caught my reflection in the mirror and cringed. My freckles were popped out in abundance and dirt smudged my cheeks. I washed my face in the restroom and walked back to the girls dorms *al naturale*. My friend stopped and her jaw dropped when she saw me. I mentally cringed again, waiting for a comment resembling, "Um, how many months has the doctor given you to live?"

Instead, she said, "Wow! You look ten years younger without makeup! I've never seen you without it. Why on earth do you wear it? You don't need it!"

Since her simple but kind encouragement, I rarely wear liquid foundation any more. In striving for that perfect look, I lost something special about myself. And I think, if you're honest, you have likely struggled with similar issues too.

I guess the bottom line is: stop taking yourself so seriously! Find a safe friend and begin sharing your failures with them. I'll predict that once you overcome the butterflies and fear, you will find an incredible freedom that will transform your life.

Finding The Wound

The landmine of perfectionism is one of those 'self-planted' landmines. Have you considered what has wounded you? Why do you strive to appear, or even be 'perfect'?

Remember, a key to discovering your wound is by understanding what you use to try to fill it. Ask God to help reveal His truth to you. Pray Psalm 139:23-24:

> *"Search me, God, and know my heart;*
> *test me and know my anxious thoughts.*
> *See if there is any offensive way in me,*
> *and lead me in the way everlasting."*

This is the key to healing and deactivating this crushing landmine. Why do you strive to be perfect? Once you've figured that out, healing is on its way. And you'll be in a position to grasp God's unconditional love for you in ways you've never seen before.

LANDMINE # 4
PEOPLE PLEASING
(All Doormats Enter Here)

Now, this landmine is especially dangerous. It's innately deceptive, more so than the others. This explosive disguises itself to look like something harmless; good, actually. But you keep dancing around it and the damage will be incalculable.

Years ago, my Grandma Fern lived at Good Shepherd Retirement Center in Little Rock, Arkansas. While living there, she was nominated to be the band director.

The Good Shepherd band usually got together once a week and rehearsed their favorite songs. They had piano, drums, tambourines and kazoos. I must say, it was one of the cutest things ever to watch their rehearsals.

Every few months they would plan a program and put on a show for their families and friends. They all wore glittery, red tops, white pants and white straw boaters while they proudly sang and played. And my Grandma sashayed around directing and teasing the audience. It was the band's chance to pretend that they were on the Lawrence Welk Show. But without the bubbles.

Well, the Fourth of July was approaching and Grandma decided that they needed to do something *big* to celebrate. This would be the show to end all shows...unless, of course, they could somehow manage to resurrect Lawrence Welk from the dead.

After weeks of mulling it over, Grandma Fern decided that there was nothing better than celebrating by performing *The Star Spangled Banner*. And nobody does bigger better than Sandi Patty.

Only one problem...no one knew how to get Sandi Patty to come that week. Or any week, for that matter. But the people had spoken. They wanted *The Star Spangled Banner* and they wanted it done by Sandi Patty.

Being a practical director, and a bit of a people-pleaser, Grandma decided the only thing to do would be lip-synch Sandi Patty's rendition of *The Star Spangled Banner*...um, yeah.

Keep in mind that Grandma was in her late seventies at this point.

Well, finally the Fourth arrived with all the fanfare that the band had hoped for. Everything went off without a hitch. And then it came time for Grandma's 'solo'.

She stood up and, as the majestic strains of Sandi Patty singing began, Grandma milked it for all it was worth. Higher and higher she soared. The anticipation began to build. The audience was captivated with her facial expressions as she enjoyed the limelight. She threw her shoulders back and moved her mouth with gusto as the ending approached.

"America!" The musical modulations began reaching higher and higher. "America!" Even higher! "America!"

Then the tape broke.

Grandma was left stranded with her mouth hanging open for the big finish. When she realized the music wasn't coming back, she gave a little smile, blushed, shrugged and sat back down.

After the show was over, a white haired elderly woman with a walker feebly approached Grandma Fern. She reached out a blue-veined, weathered hand and grabbed Grandma's own.

"What a wonderful program! But I need to ask..."

Grandma replied, "Yes?"

The old woman shook her head. "Why on earth did you stop, sweetie? You were almost to the end!"

Confession Is Good For The Soul

Okay, my friend. You know what needs to be done. You read the title to this new section and the unease began to slither through your stomach. I want you to say it with me: Hi, my name is _____ and I'm a people-pleaser.

I understand. Really I do. I'm one too. Even beyond the perfectionism and depression, people-pleasing is the one thing that remains a thorn in my side.

At one point, my people pleasing was so bad (and weird) that I couldn't even express my own tastes for fear of someone thinking I was odd. One day, my friends were chatting about how much they loved fresh tomatoes. They asked me, "Don't you love them, Tara?" I replied, "Oh, of course! There's nothing as good a fresh tomato."

Confession: I hate tomatoes with a passion.

Why did I lie? Especially over something so trivial? Because I craved acceptance. I needed their love. And I mistakenly thought that disagreement led to loss of love.

At that time in my life, I did anything that anyone asked me to do. If a deacon said the sanctuary windows needed to be washed at midnight, guess who was down at the church in the middle of night with Windex in hand?

What causes someone to be such a doormat?

The Threads That Make The Mat

First, we need to look at the behavior of a classic people-pleaser:

- Sensitive to the needs of others
- Considered kind and accessible
- Giving of time
- Going the extra mile for others
- Saying 'yes' when presented with requests of their time and talents
  - Stop here. You might be thinking, "Uh, this sounds pretty good to me. Pretty Christ-like, actually. Aren't we supposed to be like this? Serving and giving?"
  - Well, yes and no. You see these behaviors look and sound really good. Superb actually. But in order to diagnose people-pleasing (aka approval addiction) you have to look beyond the surface. Here is the flip side to these behaviors:
- So sensitive to the needs of others that they neglect their own needs.
- Appearing 'kind'; serving with a smile but filled with resentment, anger and feeling trapped on the inside.
- Over-extending themselves to the point of exhaustion and/or to the detriment of their families.
- Becoming a slave to people's expectations (or perceived expectations)
- The inability to say 'no'

It's starting to look a little more murky now, isn't it? In addition, I would add 'the need for constant approval' to the above list.

A Servant's Heart

Comedian Tim Hawkins shares about the language that Christians often use. "Phrases like 'Man, you have a servant's heart'...I hate it when people tell me I have a servant's heart.

What that means is, 'Hey man, you need to start stacking chairs.' Having a servant's heart means you're a pushover!"

Though his thoughts make me giggle, I believe Tim is right more often than not. You see, people pleasing can be extra difficult to diagnose within the realms of church. Although I'm loathe to say it, Christians are unwittingly some of the harshest taskmasters of folks who can't say 'no'. The reason being, unwise believers will take scriptures and twist them out of context to try to manipulate others into performing tasks that help them complete their own agenda.

Here are some examples:

> *Matthew 5:42*
> *Give to him who keeps on begging from you, and do not turn away from him who would borrow from you.*
>
> *Proverbs 21:26*
> *…the righteous gives and does not hold back.*
>
> *Luke 6:30*
> *Give to everyone who asks of you, and whoever takes away what is yours, do not demand it back.*

These verses sound good and right. And they are. However, manipulators will take these verses and focus on the 'doing' instead of the motivation. They breathe these verses down the necks of their brothers and heap guilt upon them if they think of saying 'no'. Taking God's Holy Word and using it to try to manipulate your brothers is called *spiritual abuse*.

God wants us to give from a heart of love. A cheerful heart is a response to our Savior's love towards us. If we are doing something out of guilt, we have lost our reward. (And consequently our joy is replaced with resentment, anger and bitterness…that empty victory we've been talking so much about.) Speaking from experience, that is a miserable way to live.

Notice the underlined portion of Deuteronomy 15:

"Give generously to him and do so without a grudging heart; then because of this the Lord your God will bless you in all your work and in everything you put your hand to." ~Deuteronomy 15:10

"Whatever you do, do your work heartily, as for the Lord rather than for men." ~ Colossians 3:23

I have a sneaking suspicion that God really doesn't care one whit for all of our good deeds, since as He himself said, our best is 'like filthy rags' in His eyes. But what He does want is a heart that is totally abandoned to Him. And the really cool thing about that is, when we love God with every fiber of our being, we love each other and don't consider those good works as an intrusion. Those acts of kindness are an outpouring from spirit that is overflowing.

Looking at it Another Way

Is this still a bit hazy for you? I understand. It can be a lot to consider and is kind of 'inside-out' approach to service.

The best learned lessons in life come from children. I heard a mother recently scold her child and her words illustrate our topic perfectly. After telling her son five times to clean his room, the mother became frustrated. "Listen to me! You are going to clean this pig-sty right now and YOU'RE GOING TO ENJOY IT!" The little boy crossed his arms with a belligerent pout and muttered, "Fine! I'll clean it. But on the inside I will NOT be happy about it."

The little son did clean his room but with a bad attitude and lots of anger. Did the mother get what she wanted? Yes and no. The 'act' was performed; the room was clean. But her son's attitude made the whole process miserable and filled their home with tension and storm clouds.

Most mothers I know don't just want their kids to obey. They want them to obey because the kids *want* to obey. They want their children to love them so much that helping is a joy.

Jesus put it best when he quoted His own Daddy's words in Matthew 9:13...

> *"Now go and learn the meaning of this Scripture: 'I want you to show mercy, not offer sacrifices.'"* (NLT)

In other words, He was saying "I don't want you to just have a clean room; I want you to love me and show that love to others."

Big difference!

A Personal Example

One Christmas, I was asked to sing a solo for the choir cantata. I had been struggling with lots of allergy problems and the song in question had a huge interval leap that had a high note landing in the upper atmosphere. Knowing it would be hard to pull off with my current voice problems, I asked the director if I could rework the melody in that phrase and opt for a lower note. He happily agreed.

Another choir member came up to me after rehearsal and began fussing at me for not taking the high note. "But that song is so beautiful with that big high note in the middle of it! You've got to do it the way it's written." Now, I'm ornery enough that when someone tells me I have to do something, I immediately want to do the opposite. Oblivious to my irritation, he continued, "Don't you trust God to help you hit that note?"

Ooooo, he played the God card. My determination to do what was best for me began to falter. Was I not trusting God to help me? Maybe I wasn't looking at this from the right spiritual angle. Was I doubting God?

Then this man landed the final blow in my spirit. He said, "If you love God, you can claim Philippians 4:13. 'I can do all things through Christ who strengthens me.' " He smiled and patted me on the shoulder before walking away. I stood rooted to the spot wrestling in indecision.

The evening of the cantata I was filled with anxiety and doubt. I decided that this man made a valid point, and more than anything else, I didn't want to let anyone in choir down. So I went up for the high note...and cracked. I wanted to crawl under the pew in embarrassment. I sat down with a red face and begged Jesus to come back immediately.

Can you see what this guy did to manipulate me? First, he tried to fix things the way he thought they should be. He refused to understand my reasons. He questioned my faith in God and then used scripture to manipulate me into doing something I knew I couldn't do. He played the God-card. A sure sign of spiritual abuse.

To all you people-pleasers out there, take heart! We are going to explore this in much more depth in part two. We'll learn why we have this compulsive need to make others happy and we'll work on tools to help you overcome this addiction.

And to all you 'pushers' out there, remember that God is God and you are not. Give the Savior a chance to work on your friends. You don't have to manipulate to see things accomplished.

And maybe, just maybe, God is calling you to do that job you are wanting your friend to do for you. Hang with me here. You are loved and we will learn more in section two.

People Pleasing Section 2: Why We Wear the Mask

"Stop regarding man in whose nostrils is breath, for of what account is he?"
~Isaiah 2:22 ESV

Okay, so we looked at some uncomfortable stuff in Part One; thanks for hanging with me. The ride might be a bit bumpy but keep hanging on. The end result will be so worth it.

If you are still a bit confused about whether your 'works' are for Jesus or a result of being an approval addict, here's a simple checklist to find the truth: (Hint: This won't work unless you're honest!)

- When was the last time you said 'no' to a request?
- Do you ever feel responsible for the mood of others?
- Do you feel like it is your responsibility to keep others happy?
- Do you often find yourself responsible for tasks that you really don't want to do?

- Do you feel uneasy about the decisions you've made until you receive approval from others?
- Do you find yourself bending over backwards to get people to like you? Even if you don't really like them?
- When was the last time you said no to someone without feeling the need to explain yourself?
- Have you ever had an opinion different from your group of peers but kept your opinion quiet because you feared rejection?
- Do you ever feel resentment towards people who make requests of your time and/or talent?
- After being at a party or other social event, do you replay conversations you had with others over and over in your mind?
- Do you constantly worry that something you said might have offended someone?

I can't speak for you, but this list makes me squirm like a worm in hot ashes; mainly, because at one time in life, I could check a big 'YES' next to all of these questions.

So why do these behaviors develop? The answers are multi-faceted and varied but we can touch on a few main ones right now. Just remember this list isn't exhaustive.

Unmet emotional needs. The root problem for most people-pleasers, and I would daresay for all humans, is the desire to be loved unconditionally. It's natural. And when we feel like we aren't loved, we try to do what we can to earn that love. Basically, we will bend over backward trying to earn approval, somehow thinking that approval equals unconditional love. However, approval and love are not the same thing.

Being taught from a young age that obedience is more important than feelings (confusing God's instructions

with man's). When I was little and in Sunday School, I was taught a song O-B-E-D-I-E-N-C-E. It used to drive my Dad crazy because my brother and I would sing it at the top of our lungs while doing things that we knew we weren't supposed to; primarily, sliding down the stairs on the couch cushions. Dad would shake his head and said, "Somehow, I think you two are missing the point of the song!"

Anyone who has spent much time in church from an early age has heard the verses about obedience. Abraham obeyed God. Joseph obeyed. Jesus obeyed. Jesus even said, "If you love me, you will do what I say." Obedience is crucial and critical to walking with God. (And consequently, having a happy life.)

However, the problem comes when we switch God's commands for people's commands. Just because someone is saved, or a Christian leader, does not mean that they are declaring God's plans for your life. Jesus even mentioned this problem in Matthew 23. He was chewing out the Pharisees, and in verse 4, He declared, *"They [Israel's spiritual leaders] tie up heavy loads and put them on men's shoulders, but they themselves are not willing to lift a finger to move them."* (NIV)

In addition, many believers are down on 'emotions'. Yes, our emotions can lead us astray. If we make knee-jerk decisions based on fear, temporary moods or anger, it can have disastrous results. But, I would contend that emotions can also be a valuable tool. After all, God created them. Jesus was known to weep, to react in anger...not to mention all the great people of faith who were moved to good works because of their emotions. (Consider Nehemiah, all those who came to Jesus begging healing for their loved ones, Joel, King Hezekiah, Isaiah and David, just to name a few.)

If someone is informing you what God demands, but unease begins to fill your soul, don't discount it. It might be the Holy Spirit telling you that this is not His plan for you. Only much time spent in prayer and Bible study will help you discover the answer.

Result of abuse, whether it is physical, emotional or spiritual. When a person has been abused in any form or fashion, they often feel that the safest course is the path of least resistance. Rather than argue, they will humbly submit to any demands or requests placed upon them. Rather than confront and risk further pain, they submit, thinking this will protect them. Instead, the opposite is true. It only subjects them to further abuse.

Insecurity and low self-esteem. These two issues work hand-in-hand with the need for unconditional love and approval.

Super sensitive to others needs. Empathy is a wonderful gift. Being able to put yourself in the shoes of others and their struggles can be a beautiful, compassionate thing. However, too much empathy, including an overactive imagination, will create worry where none exists. Disaster scenarios will bombard your mind when you consider saying 'no'. The result? To say 'yes' to help others avoid pain.

What we tend to forget is that pain helps us grow. It's impossible to develop into a mature Christian or a complete adult without conflict, pain and struggle. Sometimes saying 'yes' to someone is enabling them to stay immature. It is never okay for other people to manipulate your decisions by using 'emotional blackmail'.

I Refuse To Be A Victim!

Some psychologists say that people pleasing is an addiction. It sure did feel that way to me when I was at my worst. The thing about addictions is that it is impossible for them to grow unless they are fed; meaning, we have to be proactively engaging in those behaviors.

If we're not careful here, we could easily play the victim. It is easy to blame those that constantly make demands from us.

I well remember that feeling of being trapped. And in many ways, I was. *But*, I always had the ability to say 'no'. I just chose not to. The truth is we teach people how to treat us.

I've learned this the hard way. If you refuse to stand up for yourself, to break the cycle, you can and will eventually be plagued with anxiety, worry, exhaustion, depression, damage to your personal relationships or living in martyrdom. And yes, it's possible to suffer from this whole list at one time!

We've already talked some about exhaustion and depression, but let's look for a moment at martyrdom and damage to personal relationships.

Resentment and Martyrdom. Have you ever been around a self-proclaimed martyr? Yeah, they are no fun. The whole 'Woe is me' scenario gets really old. Martyrdom wallows in being the victim. It's a choice.

I love the following quote by C.S. Lewis*:*

> *"If you are really going to try to meet all the demands made on the natural self, it will not have enough left over to live on...In the end, you will either give up trying to be good, or else become one of those people who, as they say, 'live for others' but always in a discontented, grumbling way—always making a martyr of yourself. And once you have become that you will be a far greater pest to anyone who has to live with you than you would have been if you had remained frankly selfish."*

This can be a little more tricky than it sounds though. Martyrdom is not always a big showy gesture. Instead, it can be trickles of resentment and anger over requests but doing them anyways. A pesky bad attitude that begins to mar your service. Like a forest fire, it starts subtly but soon grows into an inferno.

Damage to personal relationships. You know what many of us forget? Our family and friends are a ministry too.

People-pleasing means that overextending yourself becomes a way of life. This, in turn, damages our most important relationships by starving them of the time and attention they need to stay strong. We get so busy running around helping others, than our own families become neglected; starving for a scrap of our attention and love.

You know what happens when we neglect our families to bend-over backwards for others? Our children and spouse become resentful. They may struggle with anger or begin acting out for attention. Some people find than any attention is good attention. Super sensitive children can become moody, depressed or withdrawn.

Your loved ones may begin looking for approval from others as well. People-pleasing, drug use, depression...the list can keep growing.

Can you see the ripple effect beginning to form here?

In a Nutshell

I recently found this quote by a Christian counselor who brutally cuts to the wound behind people pleasing:

> *"The root of people pleasing is not love; it is fear and pride. Fear that people won't like us. Fear of rejection. Fear of failure. And pride in the sense that, although we are breaking our backs "doing" for other people, we are feasting solely on the payback of their approval. We need people to focus on us, and we will go to exhausting lengths to have that need met. It is entirely self-serving...the opposite of what the Bible instructs. 'People pleasing' and 'Biblical serving' cannot be same thing. Where Biblical serving reaps immediate and eternal rewards, people pleasing is detrimental to both our emotional and spiritual health."*

Author and former people pleaser Nancy Kennedy puts it this way:

"It's one thing to humble yourself as a servant; it is quite another to reduce yourself to doing anything just to be thought of as nice. The truth is [people pleasing] isn't nice. It isn't genuine. It's narcissistic and dishonest. It's other-centered actions with self-centered motives. 'I'm nice so you'll like me.' That's not nice; that's sick."

Ouch! Are my toes the only ones that are smashed here? In feeding our people pleasing tendencies, we begin to seek the will of people over the will of God for our lives. At it's worst, it's idol worship: putting someone or something else before our Savior. Now that hurts!

In the middle of uncovering my own struggle with this, I realized that my actions were telling Jesus that what everyone else thought about me was more important than what He thought. And I was so ashamed.

Listen very carefully here: people did not die to save you. Jesus did. He is the One that you owe a debt to. No one else. Anything less than total devotion to Him will cause you pain and sorrow.

Okay, my toes can't take much more today. So we've looked at the reasons why we struggle with the need to please people and the danger that can develop from continuing.

But here is the good news: you can break the cycle. Your condition does not have to be your conclusion. After your toes have recovered from being stepped on, jump over to section three and we will learn how to disarm this landmine.

Hollow Victory · 167

People Pleasing Section 3: From Doormat to Tapestry

"You have to please only Jesus. And he is pleased with you. Not with your masks."

~Steve Brown

I love the Casting Crowns' song "Stained-Glass Masquerade"; probably, because more often than not, that song is about me. About the ways I try to hide. And it reminds me how much freedom I forfeit when I'm too scared to be myself.

It's especially a shame when I realize just what Jesus gave up to purchase my freedom. The pain, the anguish, the humility...and yet I often throw that freedom away with both hands and cower in fear.

I sincerely doubt that living in fear is unique only to me. I have a suspicion that it plagues most of us at one time or another. When we are overcome with fear, what is the natural response? To hide.

And within our churches, we tend to hide behind masks. The "I've-got-it-together" mask. The "victory" mask. I'm not messy. No sir, not me. For some reason, we think that when we give our lives to Christ, we automatically become perfect and life is a bed of roses and unencumbered bliss.

But we're not. We still have to work on our 'stuff'. The only difference is that now we have a Savior who will reveal our innermost heart to us in a brand new way. He helps us, He guides us...but we still have to try to learn and apply it. He won't force us.

"God is our one and only source of transforming truth. Deep inside in the secret places we are most vulnerable to lies." ~Beth Moore

But just like "Stained-Glass Masquerade" implies, our churches are full of believers scared to be honest about who they are and what they struggle with. Church should be the one safe place we have to come in all our brokenness and honesty, yet be loved and encouraged by the hands and feet of Jesus. Yet, we are filled with pride. We don't want the deacon to know about our pornography addiction. We don't want our sister to know that we struggle with alcohol. Whatever the problem is, we hide, because of pride, and the masquerade continues.

"When the requirement for acceptance in any particular group is to think certain thoughts, to act in certain way, and to fit in certain molds---and we don't think or act that way to fit the mold---we tend to fake it. We put on a mask that says, 'I'm just like you. Now, will you please love me and accept me?' I can think of hardly anything that will kill your joy and freedom more than wearing a mask geared to get others to accept you because you are acting like them...in many cases, the most dishonest hour of the week is the hour we spend at church." ~Steve Brown

Simply put, the masks we wear kills the freedom that Christ died to give us.

Moving from Doormat to Tapestry

So how do we disarm the landmine of people-pleasing? It takes work, awareness and time. Remember, Rome wasn't built in a day and neither were you.

1. Start asking yourself, "What's my motivation?"

When presented with a request of your time or resources, stop and ask yourself, "Why am I doing this? Is it because I really want to help out or because I'm afraid they'll be mad at me if I don't?" Dig deep. Stare unflinching into your heart.

2. Know that not everyone will like you.

It doesn't get any plainer than this. Not everyone will think you're the bomb.com. (Yes, I borrowed that phrase from my daughter.) Accept it. This is a big step forward in your path to freedom. You cannot control what others do or think about you. So stop trying. And yes, it sounds easier than it is.

3. You must get your self-worth from Jesus Christ.

This is the key. If you lose it here, you will never break free. Steve Brown hits the nail on the head in his book *A Scandalous Freedom*:

> *"It is very important that you get your self-image from Jesus. He will never lie to you, and he will always love you. Don't ask your enemy to tell you the truth about yourself. The enemy will use the opportunity to tell you that you're ugly...instead, go to Jesus and ask him. He loves you and will tell you the absolute truth. He will always temper that truth with his kindness and his grace, and nothing he shows you will change the way he feels about you. You will always be valuable to him...and ultimately, only He determines value. Once you know two things---his unconditional love and the truth about yourself---you will rest easy. And you will be free."*

Only God can love us unconditionally the way our heart desires to be loved. People can never do that. Learn from my own mistakes: seeking unconditional love in conditional people will leave you damaged and wounded every single time.

4. Learn to set boundaries.
Finding and establishing your boundaries will be the turning point in breaking the cycle. We are going to need to look at this one in depth.

Boundaries...What Type Are You?

Let's start by thinking of a fence or wall. What is it's purpose? To keep the good things in and the bad things out, right?

Let's list as many types of fences or walls as we can think of: barbed wire, picket, concrete, brick...and of course, there is always the lack of fence called 'free range'.

I have a friend who has no problems with people pleasing; instead, she is a bit callous and guarded, to say the least. She once told me that she's a twelve foot tall concrete wall with barbed wire on top and cannons positioned every five feet!

Years ago, I was one of the 'free range' fields. Anyone could come on or off. There were no boundaries, no barriers. And I was miserable. Oh, I tried erecting a fence but I didn't have the tools I needed to build. So the occasional post dotted the meadow but with no helpful results.

You don't have to be an armed fortress like my friend, but for the sake of your physical, emotional and spiritual health, you need to build some sort of boundary around yourself and the life of your family.

Let's pause here a minute and let me remind me you that having boundaries is not un-Christian. In fact, Jesus often took time away to pray and be with His Father. This was a boundary that He set up. If Jesus felt the need to establish boundaries, we should see the need for them too.

So how we do we start erecting that fence to keep the good in and the bad out?

When appropriate, you will need to start saying 'no'. Breathe in, breathe out. It's the dreaded 'n' word. If you have considered someone's request, prayed and feel it is not what God wants you to do, you will need to say 'no'. The first 'no' is always the hardest but I promise it gets easier!

Don't get me wrong: you don't have to point a finger in someone's face and scream "NO!" like a toddler. There are kind and considerate ways to respond but still maintain your boundary.

- *"I'm so sorry, but I'm afraid I won't be able to help with that."*
- *"Oh, I'm afraid I have a scheduling conflict."*
- *"I understand your position, but I've discovered that I won't be able to help that day. I wish I could."*

If someone is being pushy and/or offering unsolicited advice, you can respond with:

- *"I appreciate your opinion. You've given me something to think about."*
- *"I will pray about that. Thanks for sharing."*

This next one is a life-saver, especially if you are not sure whether it is an activity that God has given you the go-ahead to do. *It is never wrong to ask for time to pray and consider it.*

This tells the other person that you are thoughtfully considering it, but if you can't, you can share that God has not given you peace about it. It's hard for someone to argue with God's direction!

Let's stop a minute and hit on something important. Don't ask for time to think about it and then try to avoid the person with the request. Don't leave them hanging. It's rude, dishonest and could cause them quite a headache if they are in need of help. If you promise to get back to them, then do it. Let your 'yes' be 'yes' and your 'no' be 'no'. Avoidance means you are continuing in the people pleasing cycle. Honesty breaks it.

There is a lie being circled among Christians and it is this: you always have to say 'yes' if you are a believer. 'Yes' to teaching the class that no one else wants to teach; 'yes' to joining the committee that you don't have time for. And here's the rub: people say "If you really, really love the Lord, you'll *want* to say 'yes'."

A friend of mine, who happens to be a deacon's wife, was told one time that she *had* to teach the Tiny Tots class because her husband was a deacon. Never mind that my friend was already teaching the Wednesday class, running the church van *and* organizing all the music at the church.

At best, this just plain wrong and at worst, it's a form of spiritual abuse. Sometimes it *is* biblical and right to say 'no'. What if God doesn't want you teach that class, because He is calling you to teach a different group of children down the road who will need you in ways that you can't see? What if God wants Brother 'So-and-So' to join that committee because he is much better equipped to do it than you are?

Our measuring standard should never be "What will others think of me if I don't?". Our standard should always come back to "Lord, do you want me to do this?". He gives each of us different strengths and abilities and let's face it...we can't do our own job very well if we are trying to do everybody else's job too!

Pray first, speak second. And never say 'yes' if you don't feel God's peace about it. Just say no!

For those who consider a 'no' tantamount to suicide, practice on someone. Find a person you trust and have them practice different scenarios on you, with you responding with thoughtful and kind 'no's.

Just An Aside Here...

Have you ever been around a two-year old? What is their favorite word? Uh-huh...'no'. Those little ankle biters have learned their 'no' carries power, so they try to use it as much as possible to see how far it will stretch.

When I discovered the power of 'no' in my twenties, I went a little bit berserk. I started saying 'no' to everything! I sounded just like my little niece who uses the word 'no' like most people use air to breathe.

But I eventually chilled out and got back into a healthy balance. If you are the spouse or loved one of someone learning to establish boundaries, they might develop the toddler 'no's for a time. Don't stress! It will pass.

The Probability Factor

Here is the great news: after I learned to finally say 'no', most people were fine with it. I gave myself too much credit for thinking that I was everyone's answer to prayer. Overall, the response was positive and I learned to stop fearing being honest. And here's the cool thing: I watched my loved ones learn to be more honest too. We started a new cycle...a cycle of prayer, consideration and honesty.

You're probably not going to run into too much trouble once you learn how to say 'no' in a kind manner.

Safe and Unsafe People

However, there are a few pickles in every patch. On occasion, you may run into a classic abuser: someone who wants what you can provide and they wanted it yesterday. They declare it an emergency and will try all sorts of tactics to get you to concede to their demands. If you have checked your motives, prayed and do not feel like you can help, you will have to be persistent. I know this from experience. Do not try to over-explain your reasons. They will only look for a way to get around your obstacles and manipulate you. When faced with these guys, you will have to give a firm 'no' and let that be it.

They may whine, needle, plead or even attack you or your character, but stay firm. Remind yourself who you live to serve.

Again, I highly recommend Henry Cloud and John Townsend's book *Safe People*. It will help you identify those who you can trust, and those you should steer clear of. I know it sounds harsh to temporarily distance yourself from manipulators, but this is part of breaking the cycle. It's a process to learn boundaries, but when the manipulators strike again, you will be much better prepared to handle it without losing your sanity.

This can be especially tricky within the church, but remember this: there is a difference between washing your brother's feet and being his doormat.

What Is The Worst That Can Happen?

If you are continuing to struggle with exercising your freedom to say 'no', ask yourself, "What is the worst that can happen if I do?" Believe it or not, planets and star systems will not collide. The earth will not split open in a massive earthquake. Well, not because of *that* anyways.

Will people kill you? Um, not likely.

Will people pile the guilt on you? Possibly. But that's okay. This is where you remind yourself who you are living to serve...man or God? Sometimes you have to say 'no' to what seems to be good in order to receive God's best for you and your family.

Will people take away their love? Another possible yes. But anyone who says they love you because of what you do for them, probably doesn't really love you to begin with. The people who truly love you will stick with you rain or shine. And best of all, *nothing* can take away God's love from you.

Romans 8:38 declares,

> *"For I am convinced that neither death nor life, neither angels nor demons, neither the present nor the future, nor any powers, neither height nor depth, nor anything else in all creation, will be able to separate us from the love of God that is in Christ Jesus our Lord."*

To paraphrase Steve Brown in *A Scandalous Freedom*, what are people gonna do? If you are keeping your eyes on Jesus, they have no leverage. And without leverage, they have no power to keep you chained.

But, of course, *you* have to be willing to remove the chains.

People-Pleasing Section 4: Don't Take My Word for It

"But just as we have been approved by God to be entrusted with the gospel, so we speak, not to please man, but to please God who tests our hearts."
~I Thessalonians 2:4 (ESV)

Check out these insightful thoughts from my dear friend Evelyn:

Are you a people-pleaser?

Oh yes! For some reason, I always think that people don't like me. I care too much about their opinion. And I don't feel self-confident. And we *have* to think highly of ourselves because God does. Why don't we value ourselves more?

I highly recommend reading *Me, Myself and Lies*. It's all about the danger of putting ourselves down.

Do you see a pattern in churches about people-pleasing?

You know, Christians hide who they really are. We should be real. But sometimes I don't even think that *we* know who we are, because we don't act the way we do at home, when no one is looking. We should be who we are all the time…and especially at home!

~ ~ ~

Wisdom From Kay

Have you ever struggled with being a people-pleaser?

Absolutely. I'm finally trying to realize that I'm important too. I've got feelings too. I spent thirty years in a terrible marriage. He was verbally and sometimes physically abusive. But I thought staying with him was the 'right thing to do'. So I just kept sucking it up and going.

In the midst of that, how did you feel?

So lonely. Oppressed. Just oppressed. I would hide things to keep the peace. If I bought something, I knew he wouldn't want me to spend money so I would hide it from him. I hate confrontation. I stuffed all my feelings under the rug until I finally exploded. One day I just left.

How is your life different now?

I have peace of mind. I am so much happier than I've ever been. I'm learning to take care of me. I found a wonderful church and I'm doing things I never got to do before. I'm living!
    Don't get me wrong. It was really hard at first. But I took a divorce recovery class at church. I met friends….we had common ground and an outlet to share our feelings and experiences. Without their help, well, it would be too hard to do on your own. Asking for help is not a bad thing.

~ ~ ~

Cindy

Have you ever struggled with people pleasing?

Oh yes. And it has taken a very long time to overcome.

Was there anything in particular that started it?

It happened at the old church we were members of. I had a newborn, was working full time, and kept taking on more and more responsibility, teaching classes and stuff. I didn't know how to say no. And I paid the price.

How so?

Well, at that time, my oldest baby had a lot of surgeries and health concerns. I was responsible for so much as church, and became pregnant in the midst of all of it. After my second child was born, I began having panic attacks every morning. So my doctor, who is awesome, put me on medication.

Did people in your church know about it? How was that news received?

(*laughs*) Not well. Everybody disagreed with me being on meds. They all kept telling me "You just need to pray about it." Not that prayer doesn't work, but come on! It's not that simple. I did pray and God told me that I needed help! I just felt....scorned. Scorned and misunderstood.

One lady told me that "taking medication is just from Satan. Don't be taking those pills!"
We ended up changing churches after that.

How long did it take you to heal from the worst of it?

From the worst of it? About six months before I felt anywhere close to my old self. My doctor was amazing through all of it.

What advice would you give to others going through this?

Don't be ashamed or embarrassed to ask for help.

~ ~ ~

Heart Talk with Carrie

Have you ever had any issues with people-pleasing?

Yes. (*pauses*) Growing up, I had a hard relationship with my father. I could never seem to do anything to please him. I remember thinking if I could do more and be better, then he would love me. Even with my grandparents, I remember wanting to please them so badly, because I loved them. In some ways, that was very good, because it kept me out of a lot of trouble.

That's an interesting thought. I don't think I've heard anyone else mention the flip side of the benefits of being a people pleaser. It does tend to keep you on the straight and narrow.

Yep. But you know, Dad is not a Christian and still isn't a Christian. I know God's been working on him but he is still so far. I understand that. But growing up, my deepest desire was to be a daddy's girl. But all that I, and the rest of the family, got were his emotional left-overs.

When you felt that you couldn't please him, how did that make you feel?

I became very uncomfortable around men. Not just because of my dad but when I was six, I was touched inappropriately by someone. I stuffed all those emotions and feelings down. Combine that with my relationship with my father and being unsaved, and I felt completely and totally rejected. I remember even going to sleepovers and being very nervous to even be around my friend's dads, who were great guys.

Had those feelings gone back a while?

Yes, and second grade was terrible. The kids were so mean to me. But whatever they asked me to do, I would do it because I just wanted them to like me. Later on in my life, I went through a bad spell with drugs. I guess I just had this huge void inside and tried to fill it with those. All I wanted was love and a family and I felt like I had so little of both.

~ ~ ~

Prison Minister David

Have you ever had issues with people pleasing?

Yes, but you know, I finally figured out that I can't please everybody. I had to learn to like me for me. I quit trying to be somebody I'm not.

I pretended for a long time. I was doing things that others wanted me to do. It was a peer pressure type of thing. Nobody was benefiting from it.

That's interesting that you say 'nobody was benefiting from it'. I take that to mean that your efforts failed?

Yep. When I did do it, nobody was happens anyways. I guess I just wanted to fit in.

How did doing what everyone wanted you to do make you feel?
Used...and taken advantage of. And those feelings led to some bitterness and anger. After they used me, they walked off. They weren't the friends I thought they were.

~ ~ ~

Chatting with Bill

Have you ever struggled with being a people pleaser?

Yes. I've wanted to please people because it makes me feel accepted. I don't know that that is even all the issue, but I know that's part of it. I have even given things away that I really wanted to keep, partially to be accepted and partially because I know it will bring them joy.

(*smile*) Wanting to bring them joy is a good thing!

It's funny though, because my son is the same way. I've especially noticed it as he's gotten older. I can see my exact behavior running through him. Sometimes he doesn't have the time or resources to help someone but he does it anyway...often to his own detriment. I recently realized that I do the same thing.

When did you notice your people pleasing tendency?

Way back. Especially in my teens. I let people dictate what I was going to do. But then it would go on so long, those emotions would build up and then I would over-react. I went too far the other way going from no boundaries to *all* boundaries. I was very submissive. Yes, that's the best word I can think of for it. Submissive. I was a very shy student.

~ ~ ~

Wisdom from Becky

Are you a people pleaser?

I have a lot of trouble saying 'no'. Even going to a Pampered Chef party or something, I would force myself to order stuff I didn't need so the hostess wouldn't be offended. The enemy would mess with me by saying "But these people *need* you." But I realized my children needed me too and I was running all over the place trying to keep everyone happy instead of focusing on them.

Take analysis of your situation. Is what I'm doing for the glory of God?
Set boundaries. Evaluate what makes up and controls your life. This 'activity' may be good but is it for the good of God?

~ ~ ~

On the job with Ernie

You told me that in your former job, you could never please anybody. Who in particular caused you stress?

All of them! (*laughs*) All the managers. I could never make them happy.

How did that make you feel?

Inadequate. And trying to keep them happy kept me from doing my job. I would stay later to do more work. The company laid off some much needed workers and they told myself and one other worker that we would now have to do the work of fifteen engineers.

Good grief!

Yeah, it was crazy.

How long were your work days?

Usually about 7 am to 7:30 pm.

That's a really long day. What did your wife think?

She said that it had to stop. She hated seeing me working myself to death. Especially after I had the mini stroke.

When was that?

The doctor thought it was stress related. Three years later I quit. I was just so fed up with management…with people.

What advice would you give to other people pleasers?

Don't go that route! Be yourself. And do what you have to do. Looking back, I would *never* do again what I did in California. And I never felt so good as when I told the president of the company what I thought! *(smiles)*

If you were a boundary fence now, which one would you be?

Wooden railing, that some people can climb through.

~ ~ ~

Great thoughts from so many friends who have weathered the damage of people-pleasing and healed to find joy again.

To close this section, I would like to quote from Cloud and Townsend's amazing book *Boundaries*. I urge you to pick up a copy. I pray this portion will whet your appetite to learn more.

> *"Problems arise when boundaries of responsibility are confused. We are to love one another, not be one another. I can't feel your feelings for you. I can't think for you. I can't behave for you. I can't work through the disappointment that limits bring for you. In short, I can't grow for you; only you can. Likewise, you can't grow for me. The biblical mandate for our own personal growth is 'Continue to work out your salvation with fear and trembling, for it is God who works in you to will and to act according to his good purpose' (Phil. 2:12-13). You are responsible for yourself. I am responsible for myself...*
>
> *Another aspect of being responsible 'to' is not only in the giving but in the setting of limits on another's destructive and irresponsible behavior. It is not good to rescue someone from the consequences of their sin, for you will only have to do it again. You have reinforced the pattern (Prov. 19:19) It is the same principle spoken of in child rearing; it is hurtful to not have limits with others. It leads them to destruction (Prov. 23:13).*
>
> *A strong strand throughout the Bible stresses that you are to give to needs and put limits on sin. Boundaries help you do just that."*

The Wound

Are you sick of me asking you to reflect on your wound? Well too bad. It's critical and fundamental to the healing process. You have be honest and brave if you want positive change.

The landmine of people-pleasing is especially tricky and just as multi-faceted as the landmine of depression. Ask yourself, *Why do I seek other's approval and praise? What am I seeking? What is missing that I'm trying to fill?* Think about how long you've struggled with problem. Has it been in past few years or do you remember struggling with it in childhood?

Again, this process takes time and if you need additional help, feel free to contact me for additional tools and a listening ear:

>Tara@TaraJohnsonMinistries.com
>Twitter @TaraMinistry
>www.TaraJohnsonMinistries.com

Looking in the mirror can be tough but remember that Jesus is standing behind you, encouraging you to look deeply. He wants to heal you and bring into a place of joy once again. And He can't heal what we refuse to expose. Deactivate the landmine of people-pleasing and you'd find amazing freedom.

> *Lord, I ask you to open my heart to your love and light. Search me, for you know every cell of my form, every thought, every motive of my heart. Reveal my motivations to me. Make me aware. Remove any obstacle that stands between myself and You. Show me how to live to please You and not to please others. You are my Redeemer, Healer and Savior. No one else. I choose to give myself to You completely. Amen.*

Landmine # 5: Fear and Anxiety

"The opposite of love isn't hate...it's fear."
~*Carolyn Schwartz*

This landmine is petrifying. It comes on subtly and before you know it, you're consumed by it, unable to move forward. Trapped in a man-made cage that will affect every aspect of your life and relationships. Even worse, this landmine will make you forget all about your Savior and His power. You become a slave. Let's take a look...

I don't think I will forget the moment: my husband was dropping me off at our home after my music classes at UALR finished for day, when the road leading to our house was suddenly flooded with blue flashing lights.

A total of fourteen police cars crowded the intersection to our country home. Men in uniform stood around with stern faces, some talking into radios while others spoke in low tones between themselves. What on earth was going on?

As we approached the closest police car, my husband unrolled the window. The officer said, "Sorry, folks, but we've got this intersection blocked off. If you need to get to your home, you'll have to go around the back way."

My husband groaned. Going the back way added another twenty minutes to the drive. But we did it, and almost a half an hour later, we pulled up into our driveway. I could still see the flashing blue lights between the trees surrounding our home.

No sooner had my husband left to return to work than my phone rang. My friend's urgent tones exploded in the earpiece. "Tara! Are you home? Are you okay? I've been so worried about you!"

I scratched my head in confusion. "What on earth are you talking about? I'm fine. What's going on?"

Her tone of exasperation crackled over the landline. "Haven't you heard? An escaped convict is holding your neighbors hostage!"

What? I raced to the television and sure enough, a guy with squirrels juggling knives in his head was holding our neighbors two houses down hostage while the police tried to reason with him.

Waves of electricity skittered up my spine. I swallowed in terror. I was home, completely alone, with only my sleeping dog for protection.

My heart pounded in my ears. Well, no one was taking me down easy. No, sir! I raced into the bedroom and reached up into the top of closest where my husband kept his guns. My fingertips rested on cool metal and I pulled the first object I touched down and into my palm.

I grew up knowing the basics of shooting. I vaguely remembered my Daddy teaching me how to load a handgun, turn off the safety, focus and shoot. I said a quick prayer for God to refresh my memory of anything I might need to know when I faced the criminal that was sure to bust down my door any moment.

For two hours, I sat in shadowy corners of my home, the handgun cradled in my right palm, ready for action. Every few minutes I crept with the gun pointed up, near my shoulder as I warily peeked around my curtains to view the yard. Jack Bauer couldn't have been any better than I was at that moment. Keifer Sutherland, eat your heart out!

After several hours, I noticed the blue flashing lights disappear from between the tree line. I turned on the news to hear that the escape convict had been apprehended and taken into custody. I breathed a shaky sigh of relief. Thank you, Lord!

The front doorknob rattled as my husband walked in front work. He was met with a slightly hysterical but proud wife.

"Honey, an escaped convict was holding the neighbors hostage! That was the reason for all the police cars! And church members have been calling and freaking out. But I defended our home! I worked all afternoon and they caught him and...." My chest swelled in pride. "I did it, Hon!" He glanced down at the gun in my hand.

"See? I even got out the handgun! I was ready and God took care of me!"

A smile twitched his mouth as he looked at the gun in my hand. "Good job, Columbo. Did you happen to notice which of the handguns you grabbed?"

Confused, I looked down at the metal in my fingers. My gaze sharpened as I read the inscription. *Daisy*.

He burst out laughing. "Good job, Jack Bauer! You tried to defend our home with a bb gun!"

Flabbergasted, I struggled for a reply. "Uh, well, I could have shot his eyes out anyways!"

Yes, I was embarrassed and a tad bit mortified at my stupidity. I take no great pleasure in sharing my less-than-shining moment with you. I wondered later how on earth I could have missed such an important detail. Really? A BB gun?

But that's the thing about fear. It warps your perception, your situation and what outcome to expect. And it robs you of your peace of mind.

Let's learn why this landmine robs you of victorious living.

Fear and Anxiety Section 2: Shaking from the Inside Out

Picture this: You are out with your buddies. Twelve of them to be exact. And you're on a boat in the middle of a humongous lake. Sounds pretty nice, huh?

Exhausted from a day of hard work out in the hot sun, you are ready for some major R and R. Working as a team, you set sail and launch to head out to the far side of the sparkling waters. You can feel the wind in your face as it's invisible fingers push the boat farther and farther out. Before long, the sun begins to set, turning the blue skies into an orange and rust-streaked beauty just before fading into inky darkness. The chatter and teasing from your friends melts away your anxiety from the day's labor.

Suddenly, the wind increases and the smell of rain permeates the air. One flash of lightening. Then another. A boom of thunder makes everyone jump in panic. As you look up, another streak of lightening and crash of thunder seems to split the sky just before it begins pouring. Not just a drenching but the hardest rain you've ever witnessed. You're soaked through your clothes in less than a minute.

Hollow Victory · 193

The wind begins tossing your boat around like a ragdoll. Your friends fall over with the tilting ship; some staggering and others falling and grasping ropes that are billowing in the windy torrent. One wave comes up over the left side of the boat, drenching your friends even further. The boat tilts violently and a wave splashes over the other side. In the chaos, you can barely hear your own voice screaming, "Help! We've got to let down the sails!"

Your friends stumble to help while your slick fingers grasp the rough rope. Pain slices into your fingers as you pull, but no about of strain seems to be able to fight the wind. Your heart feels like it is in your throat. What is happening?

One of your buddies screams, "We're taking on water! We're going to drown!"

A sob of panic chokes you as the lightening illuminates the terror on the faces of your friends. Surely your lives won't end like this...will it? Drown together in a simple outing?

With a start, you realize one of your friends is down below the ship's deck. Slipping and sliding, you run to the stairs. Behind you, panicked screams mingle with the crash of thunder overhead. Chaos and paralyzing fear seem to be soaked into your bones.

Stumbling down the steps and panting heavily, you find your friend sleeping calmly on a pillow. You scream, "Jesus! Don't you care that we are going to die out here? Help us!"

Blinking away the heaviness of sleep, Jesus rises slowly and calmly. What is wrong with Him? Doesn't He get it? Everyone was mere moments away from death.

You stumble back up the slick, wet wood steps and scramble to help your friends. You're vaguely aware of Jesus walking calmly to the edge of the boat. Even amid the torrent of screams and crashes, you can hear His commanding voice split the air.

"Peace! Be still!" The wind that was slicing rain into your skin like bullets suddenly stops. The lightening and thunder cease. The rain seems to melt into oblivion. No one moves.

No one is capable of it. The only sound comes from the creaking wood of the boat as it rocks gently back and forth in the suddenly calm water.

Your breath hitches in your throat as you try to comprehend the change around you. In the moonlight, Jesus turns around and looks into your eyes with a wistful smile. Quietly, he asks, "Why were you so afraid? Do you still have no faith?"

Does this story sound familiar? To many of you, it should. It's taken straight out of Mark 4:35-41. It's one thing to read this passage as an innocent bystander. It's quite another to put yourself directly into the thoughts of the disciples. Terror, panic, fear unlike anything they had known before had their knees knocking together. Have you ever been that afraid?

I've read this passage dozens of times and wondered why on earth they were so freaked out. Did they just forget Jesus, the Creator of the Universe, was with them? Seems like that would be a hard thing to forget.

The disciples either forgot who was on the boat with them or they never really understood who He was to begin with.

And that, my friends, is the root of our fear.

Ironic, Isn't It?

Our enemy is always waiting to drive us crazy. When I was expecting my first child, I watched Little House on the Prairie a lot. Almost every episode was about a baby dying or some woman dying in child birth. Talk about bad timing!

Have you noticed that every time you start a new diet, commercials for Big Macs and Pizza Hut seem to taunt you? So you think that it's either eat down the refrigerate or be committed. Satan's tactics are never knew...just aggravating.

One of his primary tactics is to try to make you afraid. He does this in two ways: *oppression from the outside* or *obsession from the inside*. Sometimes we are scared because we've lived through bad circumstances before and fear the same outcome. Other times, we worry about things that likely will never, ever happen yet we obsess about the *what ifs* and *coulds*. In either case, our faith and our peace of mind rattle and seem to crumble in ashes around us.

The hard thing about identifying fear is that it isn't always a knee knocking, heart racing kind of thing. It can be much more subtle than that. Let's list different things that we are often afraid of:

- death
- **physical harm to you or your loved ones**
- **emotional harm**
- **loss of loved ones**
- **unable to control outcomes**
- **loss of love**
- **abandonment**
- **being wrong**
- **others witnessing your failure**
- **breaking out of your comfort zone**
- **depending on others**
- **being alone**

Physical and emotional harm seem fairly obvious. What we stand to lose is clear and devastating. However, the others are a big more tricky because the outcome is unclear.

Take, for instance, having others witness you fail. Is it the failing that is so bad, or the hit to your pride that you're scared of? Consider the fear that comes along with breaking out of your comfort zone. Yes, things could go really badly; however, the outcome could be life-changing and triple the quality of your life. What is it that's really holding you back?

Worry Warts

Worrying is pretty odd for me. I'm usually laidback and take things in stride. I consider this easy going manner to be a simple result of trauma from being a preacher's kid. If you can't learn to adapt to change as a PK, you'll run away screaming into the night.

I have some big decisions coming up and I suppose the weight of their impact is affecting my peace of mind. And yes, I reminded myself of the words of Jesus. "Can any of you by worrying add a single hour to your life?" Well, of course not! But it doesn't hurt to try, right?

Wrong. It actually might hurt you to try to do God's job. You might end up making an unwise decision. You might get wrapped up in your knee jerk reactions and make yourself sick trying to fix things that aren't your job to fix. And you'll wreak havoc on your spirit.

In it's simplest form, worry is this: *When I worry, it means I don't trust God.*

Ouch! That one hurts. But it's true. Worry is a result of disbelief in God, His power and His promises. And the crazy thing is that I've trusted God with my eternity....so what's so hard about trusting Him with the day to day?

This morning as I kept running all possible disaster scenarios around in my head, Jesus spoke very clearly to my heart. He said "Shhhhhh. Do you trust me or not? I've got this. I can handle it. Trust me."

With that gentle reminder, peace flooded back into my soul again. And I began to reflect on all the mighty works He has done.

If the Lord can breathe the heavens into existence and take his fingertips to mold the earth, he can handle my problem.

If the Lord can part the Red Sea and allow millions to travel through on dry ground, he can handle my problem.

If the Lord can send His only Son to die so that I wouldn't be left in the dark, he can handle my problem.

Now, I'm sure you've heard the same as I have: you share your fears and someone tells you, "Well, you should just stop worrying." Mercy, if only it were that simple! If it were that easy, I wouldn't even need to be writing this section of the book. Unfortunately, the problem is much deeper than simply a matter of will power.

My pastor recently shared that most every negative emotion you can think of is rooted in fear. Imagine that! But there is a weapon of warfare against fear.

"There is no fear in love. But perfect love casts out fear." ~I John 4:18

Perfect love is your weapon! The Greek word for *'casts'* means 'to violently displace from a position gained'.

There are two things to note in this definition. First, *the fear has to gain a position*. This means that fear has to be allowed to stay there. You've allowed it to pay rent and move in. In essence, whether you realize it or not, you've made a choice to allow it to stay.

The second thing is to look at is the word *violently*. If someone burst into your house at midnight, waving around a gun and screaming threats to your spouse and children, you wouldn't simply walk and 'show them the door' like you were wrapping up a dinner party. You would violently and forcefully throw them out.

It's not enough to hope your fear goes away. You have to make a choice to violently cast it out. You have to make a decision to work on it; to root it out and not allow it to have a place in your mind anymore. Simply put, it takes work on your part.

And yes, *the battle is for your mind.*

> *"Do not be conformed to this world, but be transformed by the renewal of your mind."* ~Romans 12:2
>
> *"Finally, brothers, whatever is true, whatever is honorable, whatever is just, whatever is pure, whatever is lovely, whatever is commendable, if there is any excellence, if there is anything worthy of praise,* think *about these things."* ~Philippians 4:8
>
> *"For though we walk in the flesh, we are not waging war according to the flesh. For the weapons of our warfare are not of*

> *the flesh but have divine power to destroy strongholds. We destroy arguments and every lofty opinion raised against the knowledge of God, and take every thought captive to obey Christ..."*
> *~2 Corinthians 10:3-6*
>
> *"You keep him in perfect peace whose mind is stayed on you, because he trusts in you." ~Isaiah 26:3*

Okay, so getting back to I John 4, what does *perfect love* mean? It sounds a bit vague, doesn't it? Let's back up to I John 4:13. Keep in mind, John is writing to those who have trusted in Christ as their Savior. None of this will work unless you have surrendered your life to Him.

> *"We know that we live in him and he in us, because he has given us of his spirit. And we have seen and testify that the Father has sent his Son to be the Savior of the world. If anyone acknowledges that Jesus is the Son of God, God lives in Him and he in God. And so we know and rely on the love God has for us. God is love. Whoever lives in love lives in God, and God in him...There is no fear in love. But perfect love drives out fear..."*

I think the key to the above passage is "so we know and rely on the love God has for us". If we truly come to understand who God is in all His unbelievable, jaw-dropping, mountain-shaking, eternal power and who we are, fallen and broken but His unconditionally loved creation, our fears will begin to melt away. He loves you so much He created you. He loves you so much He gave you His only Son to die so you could go free. This is a love that is unfathomable. Notice this verse says 'we know and *rely* on the love God has for us". It's not enough to have a head knowledge. At some point, we have to connect what we know about our Father's promises and then live in faith that He will keep His promises.

As far as 'perfect' love goes, there are several different ways to look at this phrase. The most obvious would be that if we loved God perfectly, we would never really fear anything. Our trust in Him would overwhelm every situation we encounter. Death would never make us afraid because we know what awaits us beyond. There is no more condemnation for our sins. The past, the present and especially the future are held in His hands...nothing could shake our faith in Him.

However, a more accurate rendering of the word *'perfect'* would mean *'complete'* or *'mature'*. Let's face it: we're humans. We are going to struggle with fear. As much as we'd like to think that we will never doubt or be overcome by fear, I think we all know we will. We're messy creatures.

But to have 'complete' love means that we are growing to ripeness in our faith. It means that our love for Jesus is growing and we are letting Him accomplish His full work in our hearts. The closer we are to Jesus, the less likely we are to fear.

I think of my precious friend Marie. Marie is now in her eighties and has gone through some incredibly tough stuff in her life. When she hears some of the young folks talking about their fears and worries, she just smiles.

I told her once that her faith is such a beacon of light. She is unflappable! Marie laughed lightly and replied, "Honey, when you're as old as I am, you don't worry about much anymore because you've seen God prove Himself over and over to you again. You just pray and leave it with Him, knowing that He'll take care of it in His good time. It's a very good place to live in."

Marie's faith is complete and mature. She has walked with God through the mountains and through the valleys and has come out smiling every time. That is 'perfect love'.

Do you see how fear plays a huge part in living a 'victorious life' that feels hollow? What's missing in this instance is complete trust in your Savior. That perfect love we've been talking about will fill that hollow void into overflowing peace.

Now we're going to forge ahead into a heavy (and common problem) among Christians: panic attacks.

Hollow Victory · 201

Fear and Anxiety Section 3: Panic Attacks

"You are asleep in bed, when suddenly a creak of the floor causes you to open your eyes in the semi-dark room. Towering over you stands the ugly sight of a huge man, wearing a stocking over his face. He has a gun pointed at your head. Suddenly, your heart races with fear. Your mouth becomes dry. Terror paralyzes you. You can see demons in his eyes. His evil lips smile in delight at having a human being under his power. Time stands still. Your racing heart is taking too much blood into your brain, feeding it an oversupply, making your mind go blank. This inability to respond, even mentally, brings a panic that causes your breathing to becomes erratic. The over-action of the heart also speedily lifts your body temperature to a point where cold sweat is forming on your brow, back, and legs.

With malicious intent, the intruder slowly moves the gun to the temple of your moistened brow. You can feel its cold barrel against your warm skin. The reality of what is happening tells you that this is no mere nightmare.

Adrenaline is being pumped throughout your body. Your mind is instinctively screaming RUN! It's the flight or fight syndrome. Yet, you dare not fight. You know that if you move, you are dead. With both hands on the gun, the cruel intruder slowly cocks the weapon. You see his white teeth grit in perverted glee. You are going to die a horrible death! Unspeakable terror grips your mind. Perspiration pours out of your flesh. Your mouth is totally dry. It's as though your heart is pounding through your chest. Your breath seems to have drained from your lungs and you can feel you eyes bulge with overwhelming dread..."

This nightmarish scenario, written by Ray Comfort in *Overcoming Panic Attacks*, is his description of what a panic attack feels like. Can you relate?

Panic attacks are often misunderstood. They are the extreme end of fear. Irrational and totally unpredictable, leaving a person incapable of functioning. It is reported that at least 20% of adult Americans, or about 60 million people, will suffer from panic attacks at some point in their lives. More than any other issue discussed thus far, panic attacks will leave you feeling like you were literally struck by a landmine. Not just spiritually, but physically.

Symptoms

Here is a list of the most commonly reported symptoms:

- *Racing heart*
- *Feeling weak, faint, or dizzy*
- *Tingling or numbness in the hands and fingers*
- *Sense of terror, of impending doom or death*
- *Sweaty or having chills*
- *Chest pains*
- *Difficulty breathing*
- *Feeling a loss of control*

I've heard it said that a panic attack feels like a heart attack. You see, the moment an attack comes on, you tend to over-breathe. You begin to hyperventilate. This brings on the host of other symptoms: shaking, sweats, chest pain, heart palpitations, and the like. All these problems begin to feed off each other. A panic attack is basically the whole fight or flight syndrome in motion.

What Causes Them?

If panic attacks only happen a handful of times, and around the same time in your life, it's likely a simple reaction to a stressful period in your life. They can be caused by physical distress, emotional distress or spiritual distress. However, frequent panic attacks may be part of depression or a more serious panic disorder. Only a doctor or trusted Christian counselor can diagnose the probable reasons.

Panic attacks are debilitating at worst and a huge nuisance at the least. But if left untreated, irrational fears called phobias can develop. Say you are in the middle of driving or you are in a crowded grocery store and you have a panic attack. So the next time you are in the store, you remembered having the panic attack. You think, *Maybe being in the grocery store around all these people triggers my panic attacks.* So the logical conclusion is to avoid the grocery store. Eventually, the pattern of avoidance and anxiety about having another attack reaching a point where the just the idea of going out triggers more panic attacks. You may begin to feel unable to leave your house. At this level, the disorder grows into agoraphobia.

Hiding In The Dark

Have you ever heard a very delusional but well-intentioned person declare, "Once you come to Jesus, your life will be care-free!" I usually have to choke back a snort of derision. To say that Christians don't have the same problems as every one is not just mis-leading...it's an out and out lie!

I know many Christians that struggle with panic attacks. They seems to bear an extra measure of shame because of them. But there is no shame in needing help. Everyone does at one time or another. Consider the words of Jesus in John 16:33:

> *"I have told you these things, so that in me you may have peace. In this world you will have trouble. But take heart! I have overcome the world."*

The amazing thing about being a believer who is suffering with panic attacks is that you have a Friend the rest of the world doesn't have. You have the ultimate Healer! Healing takes time but the God who scooped out the oceans can hold you, cradle you and guide you. He will help you as you change what needs to be changed. And before long, you'll find yourself running towards freedom once again.

> *"No discipline seems pleasant at the time, but painful. Afterwards, however, it produces a harvest of righteousness and peace for those who have been trained by it." ~Hebrews 12:11*

Later on. Afterwards. Do you know what that tells me? That the pain will end. There will come an 'afterward' to your panic attacks.

I like the way Ray Comfort puts it in *Overcoming Panic Attacks*: "When I was paralyzed through fear, I could hear myself saying, 'What's wrong with you! Pull yourself together. Have faith in God.' But I still had panic attacks. *I had to remind myself that I was no less spiritual than those who seemed to have complete victory over their fears.*"

The greatest spiritual giants of our time, Oswald Chambers and Charles Spurgeon just to name a few, struggled with irrational fear from time to time. When you hear the voice of condemnation in your head, do not give place to it. When the enemy is able to discourage you, he has you exactly where he wants you.

Even Paul was subject to fear. Let's take a look at 2 Corinthians 7:5:

"For, when we were come to Macedonia, our flesh had no rest, but we were trouble on every side; without were fightings, within were fears."

Does this describe you? Feeling beaten and whipped from the inside-out? Oh, my friend, there is hope. Ray Comfort, once again, hits the nail on the head:

"Satan fires arrows only at those who have potential for the Kingdom of God. You have great potential to be used by God in these days. Instead of saying, 'But God can't use me when I am paralyzed by fear,' say, 'Because His strength is made perfect in my weakness, God can use me for His glory because the fear I am plagued by actually keeps me in weakness. My fear makes me pray. I can't do it without Him.'"

Starving The Panic

So how can you decrease panic attacks?

First, remember what hyperventilating does? It tricks your body into thinking that you're not getting enough oxygen, when actually, your body is getting too much. Breathing techniques will help tremendously.

Breathe in through your nose and breathe out slowly through your mouth. Do this several times. This will put the correct level of oxygen back into your brain. You can also go for a brisk walk if possible. This will also even out your oxygen level. Another option is to hold your breath for a few seconds. Your body will respond, even though your mind might be racing.

Rate your attack on a scale of 1 to 10. This may be difficult to remember at first, but it's helpful. Write it down. "One" is a mild attack and "ten" is severe. "By scaling your anxiety this way, you are putting a fence around the experience so that the limits are clear...it will put you outside the attack---more like an observer. This will help give you a sense of control."

(Comfort) This also engages the more analytical part of your brain which helps ease the body back down into calmness. It will help you feel like you're not being threatened.

Cling to the promises of God. You have to remain in God's Word. This is a must. You cannot starve your spiritual man and expect all to be well. Find encouraging verses. Look up the promises of God. Memorize them. Have them infiltrate your spirit.

A friend of mine, who suffers from depression and anxiety, writes down God's promises on post-it notes and plasters them all around her at work and at home. She says His Word is her lifeline towards peace and calmness. Another friend repeats God's promises over and over to herself while she is in the midst of a panic attack. She credits this technique as being even more helpful than breathing techniques towards helping ease her panic.

Try these! It may take a time or two to get used to remembering to use these tools, but in time, they will help. Have you ever had a really bad round of bronchitis? The doctor will prescribe you antibiotics and will usually remind you that even though you won't feel better for a few days, do not stop taking your antibiotics, It's the same with panic attacks. Keep clinging to the promises of God. And when necessary, double the dosage.

If you haven't struggled with panic attacks, hold on. You're not home free yet. Next we'll look at the giants we face. And that is one subject *all* of us battle.

Fear and Anxiety Section 4: Giantaphobia

*"The LORD is with me; I will not be afraid.
What can man do to me?"*

~*Psalm 118: 6*

I wonder how it must have felt.

Standing in the middle of the mountain valley, clutching a slingshot in hand. The hopes and fears of all your countrymen riding on your young shoulders. To fail means that the entire nation becomes enslaved.

Directly across from you, a bear of a man sneers and hurls insults at you. Nine feet tall if he's an inch. He's a warrior. A trained killer. And he looks like he could snap you in half like a toothpick without ever batting an eyelash. Behind him, his countrymen holler out derogatory comments, insulting you but even worse, insulting your God.

Can you imagine what it must have been like to be David at that moment? I was recently reading I Samuel 17 and that got me thinking about giants.

And although I doubt that I'll ever have to face a physical giant who wants to rip me apart, I do have plenty of 'giants' in my life that need to be faced head on. What about you?

Maybe it's a broken relationship. An addiction that you just can't seem to break. A wayward child. A marriage that's falling apart. Depression? Illness? The loss of a loved one?

Speaking for myself, I feel ready to take on the world when I'm sitting in church, being filled with God's encouragement. That soft pew gives me a false sense of security sometimes, probably because my faith is not really being tested when I'm there. But how do we deal with giants beyond our church pew?

Measure the size of your obstacle against the size of your God. In her study *David: Seeking a Heart Like His*, Beth Moore states the importance of measuring your obstacle against the size of your God. "We tend to measure our obstacles against our own strength." That's the truth, isn't it? If we really understood the power and size of our God, I don't think our giants would even make us wince. We would face them unafraid and with total confidence in our Savior.

Jesus Himself said, "*Do not fear those who kill the body but cannot kill the soul...Are not two sparrows sold for a penny? And not one of them will fall to the ground apart from our Father. But even the hairs of your head are all numbered. Fear not, therefore; you are of more value than many sparrows.*" (Luke 12:4-7)

What threat then could possibly make us afraid?

Waving the white flag of surrender in your life isn't a good option. Why? Because usually that is based in fear. And fear is the enemy of God. "*For God hath not given us the spirit of fear; but of power, and of love, and of a sound mind.*" ~ 2 Timothy 1:7

Beware of the Eliab Syndrome. Differentiate between the voice of God and the voice of the nay-sayers. David's older brother Eliab became angry with him; he ridiculed and discouraged him. Do you have folks like that in your life? Misery loves company. Some people are only happy when others are miserable. Others may be battling their own demon of fear. Others lack faith in God. Beware what voices you listen to.

Let's take that a step further. Sometimes *you* can be the negative voice of Eliab. When you lose sight of how big God is, doubt can shake your faith. Cling to God's promises and remember what He has done in the past. He only brings victory.

The only way to conquer fear is to face it. If you don't face it, you will always fear it. And that very fear will keep you from the freedom in which God would have you live." (Steve Brown) Face what you are afraid of. If you start to get overwhelmed, take a break, breathe slowly and face it again. Steve Brown calls this process 'kissing the demon on the lips'. That's a very descriptive term!
This process brings tremendous freedom and those fears will lose their power over you.

This goes back to the entire premise of this book. You have to face pain head-on before you will ever be free of it.

"And lo, I am with you always, even to the end of the world."
~Matthew 28:20

This is one of the most precious promises of Jesus. In the above verse, replace the word 'you' with your own name. Now read it out loud. This verse has the power to give you goose bumps of amazement and joy. Because of Jesus, you can face the future unafraid.

Not too long ago, I was dealing with a wave of fear and anxiety. I had a rather important decision to make and wasn't sure what to do. The option I needed to follow scared me to death.

That day, a very dear friend called me out of the blue and said, "Tara, God has given me a word to share with you. It's burdening me. I can't put it off any longer. Every time you come to mind, I keep hearing and seeing the word 'oppression'.

I laughed inwardly to myself. Yep, that's exactly how I was feeling. Oppressed in spirit. Unsure what to do and just downright afraid to take the step forward.

She continued, "God wants you to know that He is about to do something big and new with you. Embrace it. Meditate on Isaiah 50:14. "Oppression will be far from you; you will have nothing to fear. Terror will be far removed; it will not come near you."

How this precious lady ministered to my heart! I felt God's love and promises wash over me anew. Later on, I continued reading down to verses 16 and 17: "See, it is I who created the blacksmith who fans the coals into flame and forges a weapon fit for its work...no weapon forged against you will prevail."

Don't be overcome by 'giantaphobia'. Remember that God is bigger. Fear and worry mean that you don't believe God is who He says He is. That He can't do what He says He can do. Remember what He has done in the past. If He brought you through the past year, He will bring you through *this* year!

And ultimately, the battle isn't yours...it's the Lord's. He is the ultimate 'giant killer'. And the ultimate landmine destroyer.

Looking for the Wound

No landmine has the ability to debilitate more than the landmine of fear and anxiety. It's paralyzing. But the key to deactivating this landmine is to figure out your wound. What is it that has triggered your fear and anxiety? Is it one of the problems listed in the first section or something deeper?

Until you unearth the source of your fear and anxiety, this landmine will continue to explode. But as I mentioned above, God can help you. He can help you unearth the source of your pain. Will you let Him? Take a step forward and search your heart.

Compare the size of your fear against the size of your God. Ignore negativity. Cling to the promises of God. Remember, the closer you are to him, the smaller the shadows.

Hollow Victory

Embracing Healing and Transformation

Take a deep breath. Whew! We've looked at some hard stuff thus far. But you've hung with me and I know we've learned so much together. We've examined the landmines of grief, depression, perfectionism, people-pleasing, fear and anxiety: all explosives that make the victorious life feel hollow.

Have you been able to identify your wound yet? Often, it takes time but I pray that you've already been able to unearth the source of what drives you. Sometimes it takes a bit of digging around the landmines to figure out what that core explosive is. And when you discover it, you'll understand why the victorious Christian life can feel hollow.

Once you've been able to discover your wound, you will begin to understand what drives you. But what is the next step?

Surrendering your Wound

Surrender is hard. By nature, you *must* give up something. Something that you treasure highly.

When I hear the word 'surrender' I always think of war, like so many other analogies in this book. Two opposing sides battling it out until one side waves the white flag, marking their opponent as the victor.

I'm going to share something with you, but it's not to get a 'poor Tara' or to have a pity party for myself. Because it's not about me. It never has been and it never will be. (Whenever I'm tempted to believe it is, God quickly reminds me otherwise.)

During 2011 and 2012, I have been struggling with gastroparesis (paralysis of the stomach). But recently a new ailment has formed: very painful esophageal spasms. My doctor is still trying to find me some relief, but at the moment, if I eat food or sometimes even drink, sing or speak, the spasms will begin and I will choke. This past Sunday morning I woke up feeling really great. No spasms or squeezing in my throat. But after singing a special in church, the spasms started in full force. And every time I've tried to sing since then has brought much discomfort.

I'll admit I've been worried. What if I lose my ability to sing? To speak? Have you ever heard of a professional singer who choked when she sang? Well, of course there's 'choking' and then there's *choking*...

This may well be a temporary problem. I hope so! But while I was hiking one morning, I thought, "But what if it's not?"

It was tempting to pray, "Dear Lord, please just do anything...*anything* to take this problem away." Much like Paul's thorn in the flesh that was driving him crazy. But God's peace flooded my heart in a profound way. Instead, I prayed, "Lord, if You will get more glory from me in this condition, then by all means, let me keep it. If more people come to know You because of it, then I will gladly claim it. Even if it means I never get to sing again, I'm ready. I'm Yours...completely."

A strong wind suddenly cut through the hiking trail. It felt like a moment of cleansing. Anything that I've held back seemed to melt away. You know, it's hard to focus on your own suffering when you are looking straight into the eyes of Jesus.

He brought to my mind a story I recently read by Corrie Ten Boom and a visit she made to a dedicated woman of God.

> *"We arrived at her apartment by night in order to escape detection. We were in Russia (in the region of Lithuania, on the Baltic Sea). Ellen and I had climbed the steep stairs, coming through a small back door into the one-room apartment. It was jammed with furniture, evidence that the old couple had once lived in a much larger and much finer house. The old woman was lying on a small sofa, propped up by pillows. Her body was bent and twisted almost beyond recognition by the dread disease of multiple sclerosis. Her aged husband spent all his time caring for her since she was unable to move off the sofa. I walked across the room and kissed her wrinkled cheek. She tried to look up but the muscles in her neck were atrophied so she could only roll her eyes upward and smile. She raised her right hand, slowly, in jerks. It was the only part of her body she could control and with her gnarled and deformed knuckles she caressed my face. I reached over and kissed the index finger of that hand, for it was with this one finger that she had so long glorified God. Beside her couch was a vintage typewriter. Each morning her faithful husband would rise, praising the Lord. After caring for his wife's needs and feeding her a simple breakfast, he would prop her into a sitting position on the couch, placing pillows all around her so she wouldn't topple over. Then he would move that ancient black typewriter in front of her on a small table. From an old cupboard he would remove a stack of cheap yellow paper. Then, with that blessed finger, she would begin to type. All day and far into the night she would type. She translated Christian books into Russian, Latvian, and the language of her people. Always using just that one finger — peck,*

peck, peck —she typed out the pages. Portions of the Bible, the books of Billy Graham, Watchman Nee, and Corrie Ten Boom---all came from her typewriter. That was why I was there-to thank her. She was hungry to hear news about these men of God she had never met, yet whose books she had so faithfully translated. We talked about Watchman Nee, who was then in a prison in China, and I told her all I knew of his life and ministry. I also told her of the wonderful ministry of Billy Graham and of the many people who were giving their lives to the Lord. "Not only does she translate their books," her husband said as he hovered close by during our conversation, "but she prays for these men every day while she types. Sometimes it takes a long time for her finger to hit the key, or for her to get the paper in the machine, but all the time she is praying for those whose books she is working on." I looked at her wasted form on the sofa, her head pulled down and her feet curled back on her body. "Oh, Lord, why don't you heal her?" I cried inwardly. Her husband, sensing my anguish of soul, gave the answer. "God has a purpose in her sickness. Every other Christian in the city is watched by the secret police. But because she has been sick for so long, no one ever looks in on her. They leave us alone and she is the only person in all the city who can type quietly, undetected by the police." (from Tramp for the Lord)

My question for you today is, what are you holding back from God? Your children? Your spouse? Your job? Your fear? Your need for approval? We will never reach our potential in Christ until we surrender completely to the Master.

The Welcome Prison

Often I go into our local prisons to sing and share the gospel with the inmates, male and female alike. Do you know what I've discovered? Some of those guys find their prison to be a real comfort. It's safe, comparatively anyways. They are sheltered from the outside world, but mostly they are sheltered from themselves.

One inmate recently shared with me that he was scheduled to be released within the month. I smiled and replied, "Oh that's wonderful!"

Worry lines creased his forehead. He whispered, "I'm terrified. I have too much freedom out there. How can I be sure I won't turn back to the drugs again? There's no one standing over me telling me where to go and what to do. I know I'm going to fail! I want to stay in here."

My heart broke for him. For him, freedom was scary...terrifying. Aren't we like that sometimes? It's easier to stay locked in our comfortable prisons. Although miserable, we grow accustomed to it until the thought of stepping into the unknown leaves us paralyzed.

Sometimes, I think we may unwittingly step on the same landmine over and over again. Reason being, even though we're injured, it's all we know. It's a familiar type of pain. Lord, help us be brave enough to break the cycle!

Obsessing About The Cage

Once we step into the light of freedom, it's addictive. Glorious. Joyful. And the more the light exposes our wounds, the quicker we heal. It becomes a little bit easier to be real. Transparent even. We never were called to share about how awesome *we* are. We're just supposed to share about the freedom we've found in Christ.

Just a word of warning here though: sometimes, if we aren't careful, we can look back at our old cage and glorify the sin. What I mean is, we can talk about how far we fell and soon begin talking only about ourselves. We obsess about our past.

In *A Scandalous Freedom*, Steve Brown states, "One of the greatest sins Christians can commit is a constant focus on their sin. It is a far more prideful and arrogant exercise than almost anything you can do."

He continues:

> *"I remember when I found out that Donald Grey Barnhouse felt jealous of Billy Graham, that C.S. Lewis had a weird relationship with a substitute mother, that Charles Spurgeon went through months of depression and refused to preach because of it, that Martin Luther wrote anti-Semitic pamphlets, that...well, you get the idea...He [God] uses sinful and flawed human beings because those are the only kinds of human beings he has available to use.*
>
> *Whatever you think about the Bible, it doesn't contain 'puff' biographies. In fact, God has been very careful to allow us to see the greatness and the smallness of biblical characters. Throughout the Bible, we encounter heroes of the faith with major flaws, serious sin, and embarrassing failures. Adam and Eve messed things up for themselves and for the rest of us. Noah got drunk. Abraham offered his wife in return for his own safety (twice). Sarah offered her female servant to Abraham so Abraham could have a son. Jacob was a con artist. Moses was a murderer. David was an adulterer. Jeremiah was a big time failure. Rahab---an ancestor of Jesus---was a prostitute. Paul was contentious. Peter was a hypocrite."*

Don't get me wrong here. I'm not saying that we try to hide our mistakes. That isn't freedom either. We should always be honest.

But what I am saying is that instead of always pointing to 'me, me, me', every time we share our testimony, we should point to Christ as our Healer and Restorer.

Do you know what would be really refreshing? If, instead of acting like we never messed up or saying, "Woe is me! Look at what I've done to my life!", we said, "Boy, I've made some royal mistakes in my life. But you know what? I've discovered that God is crazy in love with me anyways. And He loves you like that too! Wouldn't you like to know Him?" I think people would come running to Christ. Freedom is a highly attractive gift.

My friend Eduardo Magana, missionary to Saltillo, Mexico, recently shared this simple prayer on facebook: "We seek God's presence in our lives. We should be reflecting His light so others will see Him and know that He is good. It's not about me. Lord, make me a moon, a mirror, a glass windows...whatever reflects Your Son."

I think sometimes we try to put God in a box. We analyze Him. We try to figure Him out. We come up with bullet points and charts. We make lists and rules, graphs and formulas. I believe this tricks us into thinking we have a sense of control.

But God is too big for our boxes. And honestly, the healing process can't be put into a simple checklist. It takes time. Just when you think you've got it figured out, God pulls out a trick and says, "Okay, now we need to look at this..."

Before healing can take place, we have to get a good grasp of God's precious gift...grace.

Healing and Transformation
Section 2: Understanding Grace

"We can underline our Bibles till our pens run dry without a drop of ink splattering our lives. The self-deception slithers in when we mistake appreciation for application or being touched with being changed. The tricky part is that hearing all by itself really does lend a certain satisfaction. Think about the last time you closed your eyes and listened to an instrument that nearly brought you to tears. Something similar can happen when we listen to Scripture being read or a message being taught. The hearing itself can be satisfying, and we nod our heads with genuine resonance. The Word of God, however, is meant to do more than penetrate. It's meant to activate."

~Beth Moore

Why is grace so hard to understand? It's hard for me, anyways. A simple definition of grace is getting something good that you don't deserve. It sounds easy enough until I realize the depths of my own sin. What kind of forgiveness can erase my sin as far as the east is from the west?

I once read a story about grace that impressed this concept deeply into my spirit. I'm loathe to admit I have no idea where I read it or heard it. Forgive me for not being able to share the author with you. I'll do my best to remember the gist of the story.

There was a young mother who was having a terrible time with her oldest son obeying. He would bully his little brother and sister and sulked whenever he was asked to help clean up at home. One day, the mother promised the children that if they helped her clean the house, she would take them for ice cream afterwards. The children were delighted and leapt right up to do their chores...all except for the oldest.

Seeing his bad attitude and refusal to help, the mother became frustrated and told the son, "I told you what you needed to do and you've refused. So here is what's going to happen: we are all going to go out and get ice cream, but you won't be getting any. You're going to have to come along and watch your brother and sister enjoying it."

Of course, the son was angry and pouted the entire car ride over. Sitting in the booth with her own double dip cone, she watched her three children; two happily slurping their ice cream and the other angry with his arms crossed. She realized this was a prime moment to teach them about Jesus.

She smiled at her oldest son and said, "Do you know that God gives us grace? Sometimes, He gives us good things that we don't deserve. Son, I want you to understand God's grace. Here," she held out her ice cream cone to him, "even though you should be punished, I'm going to give you my cone."

The little boy's face lit up with joy and amazement. Before she could blink, he grabbed the cone and began scarfing it down. The mother sat a little shocked at the lack remorse he showed for his earlier behavior and the glee he took in gobbling up her treat. The little stinker! She watched him licking up the drippy mint chocolate chip and became angry.

Didn't he even care about her feelings? Then, with a start, the mother realized that she had offered him grace but she was sitting and sulking in her own bad attitude. In amazement, she realized that her son accepted grace freely and happily. But she was sitting there thinking that he owed her something. That wasn't grace at all. It was a bribe.

As she watched him giggling with his siblings, she smiled. *Okay, Lord, that little demonstration wasn't for him at all, was it? It was for me. My boy understands grace. It's me who doesn't. Thank you for loving me and giving me good things, even when I don't deserve it...*

The Big Mistake

See, in understanding grace, we often make a huge mistake: we assume that God's goodness is the same as the 'goodness' of our family and friends. We wrongfully judge Him, thinking that He must judge us the way we judge ourselves.

My judgments are too unstable: either I think way too much of myself or I beat myself to a pulp when I mess up. My pendulum swings between pride and self-loathing; foolish conceit to depression. But with God, there is no variation or shadow of turning. He is love. He is stable. He is perfect.

We have horribly skewed misconceptions about who God is. Sheila Walsh puts it this way: "I wonder if what we believe about God is because of what we personally have learned about Him or based on what other people have told us about Him."

And obviously, if we don't really have a grasp on who God is, we can't really understand His grace or forgiveness either. We hide ourselves in shame and refuse to be honest with Him. Considering the price His Son paid, this must break His heart.

Stubbornly Free

My dear friend April has gone through some incredibly tough things in her life. Some of these she will tell you were her fault and some were the fault of others. But what I admire most about April is that the day she gave her life to Christ, she refused to listen to those voices of doubt any longer.

She shared with me that, during an argument, a family member brought up one of her failures from the past, a time before she met Jesus. Before any more accusations could be leveled, April stood up straight, squared her shoulders and declared in confidence, "You will *not* make me feel guilty about my past because I now live in freedom! My wounds are now badges that I proudly wear. They remind me what Jesus has saved me from and those same wounds have equipped me to help others. I will not let that negativity have a place in my heart! I'm free!"

I wanted to stand up and cheer! April 'gets' grace. As a matter of fact, she is righteously indignant about it.

Sometimes, we misunderstand grace because we think that grace means that we won't ever go through some tough stuff. This is a tragic error in our thinking!

> *"Take for instance a world champion boxer. His coach loves him to a point where he wants him above all things to be a winner. So, what does the coach do---buy him a sofa, a TV, and potato chips? No. Instead, he places weights on his shoulders and resistance against his arms. He will even look around for the toughest sparring partner he can find. If the boxer doesn't understand what his trainer is doing, if he doesn't have faith in his methods, he will get depressed and lose heart. But if he knows what's going on, he will rejoice now in the trials because he sees, through the eyes of faith, the finished product...*
>
> *Afflictions work* for *us, not against us, if we are in God's will. How is your joy when the Trainer brings the resistance your way?*
> *The joy you have will be your measuring rod."*
>
> ~Ray Comfort

Well said, Ray. Well said.

"For our light affliction, which is but for a moment, works for us a far more exceeding and eternal weight of glory."
~2 Corinthians 4:17

Show Me Your Glory

(Inspired by Max Lucado's book It's Not About Me)

If you knew you could have any wish granted, what would it be?

Well, I can tell you what Moses' wish was. He had been up on Mt. Sinai for days on end, no food or water, receiving God's holy instruction for Israel while those very same people down below were sinning, partying and doing whatever they could to rebel. (See Exodus 33.)

In the midst of all of this, what was Moses' one request? Food? Punishment for his wayward children? A request to be relieved of this awesome responsibility? Victory in battle? To be the best leader he could be?

No. Instead, he asked God, "Show me Your glory."

And God granted his request. "There is a place near me where you may stand on a rock. When my glory passes by, I will put you in a cleft in the rock and cover you with my hand until I have passed by. Then I will remove my hand and you will see my back; but my face must not be seen."

After just a glimpse of God's glory, Moses' face was so radiant that people were scared to come near him. That is a jaw dropping, mind boggling, infinitely beautiful kind of glory.

What constitutes our daily requests? The sick pray, "Lord, help me to feel better soon...". Musicians pray, "Lord, help that record label to sign me...". Writers pray, "Lord, help that publishing company to offer me a contract...." Workers pray, "Lord, help me get through this awful day of work...".

But how often do we pray, "Lord, show me Your glory"?

Because the thing is, if we ever caught just the briefest glimpse of His glory, of who He is in all His majesty, we would hit our knees in awe and our lives would never, ever be the same. And neither would the lives of those around us.

I think the key to finding freedom, living in victory and understanding grace, is to learn to think like God. That seems like a tall order, doesn't it? After all, He's *God*. We will never be able to fully grasp all that He is. Our puny brains can't take it all in. But we can learn and know the heart of God. We have to learn to look at our mistakes, wounds and prisons through the viewpoint of His light and not the darkness of our past.

So how do we learn to think from God's viewpoint? Well, I'm glad you asked...that's exactly what the next few sections are all about.

Healing and Transformation
Section 3: A Date with Jesus

There was once a married couple who had been together for twenty years. One day they drove down a long, dusty country road, leaving their home to take a trip into town to get groceries and supplies.

As they passed mile after mile of agricultural land ripe with growing corn and wheat, the wife began to think of their many years together. She thought of how she and her husband had met at their high school dance. They had fallen in love and became inseparable. Several years later they were married.

She recalled how they had held hands everywhere they went; how her heart would thunder when he came home from a long day at work and how his smile made her feel like the most beautiful woman alive.

Why, even on their trips to town, she would cuddle next to his side as they drove in his old pickup truck, talking and laughing as they journeyed together, smelling the sweet scent of hay through their open truck window.

Looking down at her lap, she noted the empty space between the two of them in the truck's front seat. Her husband drove with his strong hands on the wheel, his eyes fixed straight ahead. She began to cry.

"Why, darlin', what's wrong?" he asked gently.

"For years when we were first married, we couldn't stand to be apart. We did everything together! I even cuddled up next to you while you drove. Don't you remember?"

The husband smiled and nodded. "Yes, I remember."

A spark of anger flickered through her. "Well, don't you care that we don't cuddle on the way to town anymore?"

The husband gave her a sidelong glance and replied, "Sweetheart, I've never moved."

What's Missing?

I've heard it once said that God never moves. If He did, He would just bump into Himself.

And I know this to be true. He is immovable, unchangeable. So if there is distance between my Savior and myself, guess who moved?

I'll be honest: during the past year I have felt something lacking in my relationship with the Lord. I knew it wasn't Him. It never is. But something wasn't quite as vibrant as it used to be and I couldn't seem to put my finger what it was.

I'd confronted the landmines in my life. I read my Bible daily and prayed often during the course of each day. I was filling myself with His Word and rarely missed a worship service at church. I was doing everything I knew to do and still I felt that we were not quite connected. It just wasn't enough.

I began to wonder if there was some sort of un-confessed sin in my life. I wracked my brain and spirit trying to identify the source of my angst.

Then one morning, I opened my Bible to Psalm 46:10.

"Be still and know that I am God."

Be still? Me? I'm like a Chihuahua on steroids. That's the hardest thing to ask me to do!

Over the next week, I began to meditate on what it means to 'be still'. I believe many of us, myself included, have a form of idol worship in our lives; primarily the idol of busyness.

Now don't get me wrong here. Being busy can be very good, especially when we are busy doing God's work. Teaching Sunday school, VBS, leading worship, running the church van, sending cards and making phone calls are a vitally important part of any ministry. Not to mention the most important ministry we have, and the most time consuming---our children and spouses.

However, a certain danger begins to develop when our busyness turns into a spiritual hamster that can't get off the wheel. Let's face it…if the hamster stays on the wheel for too long, it will die!

I realized that in the hustle and bustle of all my good ministry activities, including Bible reading and prayer, I was learning about God but I wasn't spending time with God. This is a subtle but substantial difference.

I think this is not an intentional choice in most Christians. We want to learn more about God. We want to know what pleases Him, what delights Him, why He loves us…that's good! But sometimes we get so busy with wanting to know about Him that we forget to just ask Him ourselves.

It would be like having Albert Einstein in the room but you're so busy reading a book about him that you don't even notice he is there.

For several days, I racked my brain on how to remedy this. I mean, ideally, worship on Sundays is the perfect time to draw close to Jesus.

But let's be honest for a minute, shall we?

My Sundays are rarely restful. I know how it should be, but most of my Sundays follow this pattern: wake up early, get up the family, fix breakfast, help kids get ready, break up fights between the kids (because Sunday is usually the one day that satan tries his best to rile us up), get myself ready, rush to

Sunday School (usually late), juggle time between the little kids' music and actual Sunday school, play the piano for worship, prepare and sing a special, thump my children in the head during the sermon for giggling, fix lunch, clean up lunch and it's back to church again at 4:30 for choir, regular evening worship, late dinner, clean up, baths…oh, and on occasion throw in the occasional potluck as well. And that is a quiet Sunday for us.

For anyone actively involved in church, the responsibilities of music, teaching, directing, finances, etc. can end up becoming a major stresser. But we can't just bury our heads in the sand…somebody has to do them!

Finally, I threw up my hands in frustration. It wasn't working! I was going to have to be proactive and set aside time to just spend with my Savior. No distractions, no interruptions.

That's right…I scheduled a date with Jesus.

So one Friday morning, I dropped off the kids at school and headed towards my date with my Redeemer. In the early morning hours, while it was cool and quiet, I hiked up Pinnacle mountain. Pinnacle is about fifteen minutes from our home and takes about thirty minutes to hike. A perfect place to find 'stillness' with God.

I left my phone at home. I panted in the early morning quiet as I reached higher amid the sounds of scampering squirrels and chirping birds. When I reached the top, a breath-taking vista greeted me; the green valley spanning before my eyes in every direction while red-tailed hawks swooped and glided around the summit.

That morning, I sat at the top of Pinnacle Mountain and just talked with Jesus. I poured out my hopes and dreams. After sharing my heart with Him, I became quiet and just listened for His still, small voice.

And you know what? He answered.

He spoke to my heart. He called me His princess. He flooded my spirit with His peace. He told me that I needed to wait on Him for certain things that were worrying me. And He assured me that He would always love me unconditionally.

I walked down that mountain with a refreshing that I hadn't sensed in years. And it has since become the most essential part of my week.

I cherish and crave that time with Him. All week long I look forward to our 'date'. I'm learning how to be with Him and my, what a difference it makes!

Some days I've climbed to the top and grieved for the babies I lost. Sometimes I sit at the top and sing praise songs to Him. Sometimes we just chat about nothing and everything. And some things I won't share here because they are private conversations for my Savior's ears alone. But each time I walk away tangibly sensing His presence.

I know, I know. Saying that I have a 'date with Jesus' sounds a little crazy. Believe me, when I first told my husband I had a 'date with Jesus', I know he was thinking that I had squirrels juggling knives in my head. And I know that because he told me so!

But honestly, I don't care. That's what it is…a scheduled, special time with my Lord. And some amazing things have resulted from it.

One morning I reached the top and was dismayed to discover another hiker at the summit who was just waiting for someone to come by and have a nice long chat. Inwardly, I groaned. This was my special time! Surely the Lord didn't expect me to abandon Him.

But of course that was ridiculously selfish on my part. As the stranger and I began to visit, I became interested in his own story of heartbreak and loneliness and was ultimately able to introduce him to the Savior. And there have been many more ministry opportunities since that day.

Consider the beautiful words of David and Jesus:

"He who dwells in the shelter of the Most High will rest in the

shadow of the Almighty. I will say of the LORD, "He is my refuge and my fortress, my God, in whom I trust."
~ *Psalms 91:1,2*

"I lift up my eyes to the mountains---where does my help come from? My help comes from the LORD, the Maker of heaven and earth."
~ *Psalms 121: 1,2*

"I am the vine; you are the branches. If a man remains in me and I in him, he will bear much fruit; apart from me you can do nothing."
~ *John 15:5*

"You will seek me and find me, when you seek me with all your heart."
~*Jeremiah 29:13*

Several times I've thought about bringing a friend or two with me when I go hiking but then I realize that it would no longer be special alone time with Jesus…it would be time with them. I know myself---I would chatter all the way up the mountain and it would turn into a giggle fest. It wouldn't be a date with Jesus anymore but instead would turn into a girls' day out!

I'm learning to make time with Him a priority. I'm fiercely protective of it. And He continues to teach me so much: to listen, to wait, to be still, and how to have peace in the midst of the chaos twisting and turning around and inside me.

I encourage you to make a date with Jesus. It doesn't have to be a whole day or even half a day. Let's face it: many of us don't even have one hour! But even if it's just ten or fifteen minutes somewhere quiet…go on a walk, sit outside under the stars or even lock yourself in the bathroom. It doesn't matter. That's the nice thing about being omnipresent. He can be with you anywhere!

I promise you, you won't be disappointed. In fact, I would daresay that you'll wonder how you ever managed without it.

And speaking for myself, I'm falling in love with Him all over again…

The Eye-Opener

Attending church is not necessarily spending time with Jesus. Teaching a Sunday School class is not necessarily spending time with Jesus. Reaching out to the community in ministry programs is not spending time with Jesus. My friend Evelyn puts it this way: "Time spent *for* Jesus is not the same as time spent *with* him."

We spend so much time studying God, obeying God, learning more about God…but how many of us are enjoying Him? And this, I believe, is the distinct difference between having a hollow victory and living in true, breath-taking, vibrant victory.

At His Feet

Have you ever wondered which person from the Bible you are most like?

Are you a hot head like Peter? As easy-going as Joseph? Maybe you're a musician like David or great leaders like Moses and Esther.

I fear I'm much too similar to the messy people in the Bible. But next to Jesus, my heart's desire is to be like Mary of Bethany. Little is said of her. But what is mentioned has left an eternal impression upon my mind.

Not long ago, my pastor mentioned that Mary of Bethany is mentioned three different times in the Bible, and each time, she ended up at the feet of Jesus.

Here is the first instance:

> *"As Jesus and his disciples were on their way, he came to a village where a woman named Martha opened her home to him. She had*

a sister called Mary, who sat at the Lord's feet listening to what he said. But Martha was distracted by all the preparations that had to be made. She came to him and asked, 'Lord, don't you care that my sister has left me to do the work by myself? Tell her to help me!'

Martha, Martha,' the Lord answered, 'you are worried and upset about many things, but few things are needed—or indeed only one. Mary has chosen what is better, and it will not be taken away from her.' "

~Luke 10:38-42

Forget the dusting. Forget the vacuuming. Forget make a killer meal for the Son of God. Mary knew that the real treasure was sitting at Jesus' feet. She was drawn to Him like a moth to a flame. She sat at His feet to learn and to hear the Voice of truth.

The second instance occurred after her brother Lazarus had died. Beside herself with grief, Mary ran to Him when she heard he had arrived four days after her brother's passing:

"When Mary reached the place where Jesus was and saw him, she fell at his feet and said, 'Lord, if you had been here, my brother would not have died.' When Jesus saw her weeping, and the Jews who had come along with her also weeping, he was deeply moved in spirit and troubled."..."Jesus called in a loud voice, 'Lazarus, come out!' The dead man came out, his hands and feet wrapped with strips of linen, and a cloth around his face."

Imagine the rejoicing that must have followed! How Mary's heart must have thudded in shock as she watched her brother walk towards her wrapped in his grave clothes. The tears that must have streaked down her cheeks, as she flung herself at him, overcome with joy. I wonder if she looked back to see Jesus. Can't you imagine Him smiling and she returning the smile with one of her own...a smile filled with gratitude and awe?

She fell at His feet when she was overcome with sorrow and despair. And Jesus was moved to tears.

Yet the third instance might be the most precious of all.

> *"Six days before the Passover, Jesus came to Bethany, where Lazarus lived, whom Jesus had raised from the dead. Here a dinner was given in Jesus' honor. Martha served, while Lazarus was among those reclining at the table with him."*

I can smell the savory food and the chatter of people attending this special dinner. There must have been laughter, the sound of murmuring voices and the gentle thumps of dishes being served.

Amid all the hustle and bustle, I can picture Mary standing in the corner, quietly observing. I wonder if she ever felt like she was in a dream. How could her brother have been dead not long ago, yet was at this moment alive and eating next to Jesus? It was surreal.

Her eyes roved over the brotherly face she knew so well...the face that was so familiar. Then her gaze sweeps to Jesus.

Before she realizes it, a gentle sob of gratitude bursts from her chest. How can she show her love and adoration for the One who had so transformed her life?

> *"Then Mary took about a pint of pure nard, an expensive perfume; she poured it on Jesus' feet and wiped his feet with her hair. And the house was filled with the fragrance of the perfume.*
>
> *But one of his disciples, Judas Iscariot, who was later to betray him, objected, 'Why wasn't this perfume sold and the money given to the poor? It was worth a year's wages.' He did not say this because he cared about the poor but because he was a thief; as keeper of the money bag, he used to help himself to what was put into it.*

Leave her alone,' Jesus replied. 'It was intended that she should save this perfume for the day of my burial. You will always have the poor among you, but you will not always have me.' "

She fell at His feet in worship. But there's more to learn here.

Jesus had been telling His disciples over and over again that He would soon have to die. But they didn't get it. Didn't understand. You would think they were blonde or something.

But Mary understood. How was that possible?

Because she had spent her time at the feet of Jesus.

So not only did she sit at His feet to learn, to cry, to worship....but in doing so, she understood the very will of the heart of God.

And you can know the heart of God as well, my friend. Spend some time with Him and enjoy His goodness.

HEALING AND TRANSFORMATION
SECTION 4: SPEAKING & LISTENING

A friend of mine recently sighed in exasperation and said, "Sometimes I wish life came with an instruction manual." I thought for a minute and smiled before replying, "Oh, but it does! It's called the Bible!"

There are two essential components to healing and living victoriously that I cannot stress enough. We have heard the call to engage in these activities so many times that it's become like a drone in our ears. Nevertheless, their power is revolutionary and life-changing...reading God's Word and praying.

The Love Letter

To put it in its simplest terms, prayer is talking to God. Reading His Word is the way that He talks to us. Both complete the communication in our relationship. We might pray and talk all day long, but unless we hear God's response, we feel paralyzed in indecision. Conversely, we can read the Bible all day long and benefit greatly from it, but unless you are talking with your Father, something vital will be missing.

How much trouble would a marriage be in if the couple never talked? Or if one spouse talked constantly and never gave their mate a chance to a get a word in edgewise?

The Bible is more than a collection of thoughts and stories by men: it's the God-breathed, inspired, living, active Word of the Creator of the Universe. It gives hope, reveals the future, comforts, encourages and corrects. It's sharper than a sword, it's powerful, active, and reveals the attitude of our innermost person, as well as the attitudes and thoughts of others. Even more than that, though, it is a love letter from God to His kids.

Let's get honest: sometimes I can't wait to dig into my Bible study. It's a breathing, inspiring thing. I crave it like I crave water on a hot day. Other times, depending on illness, exhaustion or just a too-busy schedule, my time in God's Word can feel like a chore. A dry, dusty time in my already cramped day.

Since we are fickle, emotion-driven, unstable creatures, we have to approach our time in God's Word like physical food. Tell yourself, "If I skip my Bible time, I have to skip breakfast." This physical body will pass away; our spiritual won't. So which of the two is more important to feed? It *will* benefit you, whether you feel like it or not.

Ray Comfort words it this way:

"Each day, find somewhere quiet and thoroughly soak your soul in the Word of God. There may be times when you read through its pages with great enthusiasm, and other times when it seems dry and even boring. But food profits your body whether you enjoy it or not."

Not every meal can be a dessert bar. There must be a balance. Another important issue to be aware of is the time of day you choose to study. For years I used to read my Bible just before I went to bed. More often than not, I had to re-read a passage two or three times to get it, often bleary-eyed and yawning. After I finally realized that I'm a morning person and am worthless after 10 p.m., I switched my study time to morning right after the kids leave for school. That simple change has revolutionized my study time! Honestly, because I'm a morning person and find my best focus in the early hours, the Bible never seems dry to me anymore. (Except for maybe some of the 'begats'.)

If you feel disconnected and a bit stale in your study time, try switching up your schedule. You'll never know unless you try it! Memorize the Word. Think about it during the day. I suspect that, in time, you will think of it like a dessert instead of a plate of vegetables.

The Myth Of 'Unanswered' Prayers

I have a big issue with Garth Brooks' song *Unanswered Prayers*. God *always* answers His children; it just may not be the answer we want.

Granted, God won't answer your prayers if you are not His. The only prayer He answers from unbelievers is the prayer to be saved. And if our hearts are right, praise God, He always says 'yes' to that one! But among believers, His children, we somehow get it in our heads that just because we don't get an immediate 'yes' to our prayers, God isn't listening.

Our Father usually answers in one of three ways:

> 1. **Yes** — "This is my will and plan for you right now."

> 2. **No** — "Even though you'd like this, I can see down the road. It will bring harm to you."

> 3. **Wait a little bit longer** — "I'm leading you towards this path, but the time is not ready yet. You need to grow a bit more. I'm preparing other hearts

to take part in this and they aren't ready yet. Trust me. Be patient."

All three are answers. Some just mean that we won't get our way, at least not right away.

Jesus modeled what prayer should be in Matthew 6: 9-13:

Our Father in heaven	God is our Father, our Daddy
Hallowed be your name	His name is holy, consecrated, set apart above all others
Your kingdom come	His will is our top priority
Your will be done on earth as it is in Heaven. Give us today our daily bread.	We know you will give us all we need
Forgive us our debts	Forgiveness for daily sin that keeps us from walking in total unity with Him.
As we forgive our debtors	We forgive those who wrong us
Lead us not into temptation	Keep Your hedge of protection around us.
Deliver us from the evil one	So satan can not harm us or lead us astray

Prayer is not about us. It's not about us getting our own way. It's about putting our plans in alignment with God's perfect plan. It's about surrender and needing His guidance.

Loving On Daddy

Some of my favorite moments as a mom is when my children come up to me and say, "I love you, Mom". I didn't say it first to them. There was no other reason for their sweet words. Just a simple outpouring of love from their little hearts. I melt into a puddle every time they do that.

Have you ever just told God you love Him? No agenda, no wishes...just love. Talk to God as a Daddy, for He *is* your Daddy. (By the way, the Hebrew word *Abba* that Jesus often used when talking to His Father literally means 'Daddy'.) Crawl up into His lap and tell Him everything.

Break free from the same old patterns of praying. We've all done it. Prayer will seem like a dry chore unless we talk to God like our Daddy. How would you feel if your child pulled a pre-written statement and recited it to you day after day? Yeah, that would stink.

Power Steering

Prayer is power. I've seen God do amazing things time after time when His people believe in Him and pray.

Last Wednesday evening, our little family was in the church parking lot visiting with friends. Amid the teasing chatter and conversation, the hour slipped by. Before we knew it, darkness had descended and mosquitoes had us slapping the little nuisances away. After waving goodbye to our church family, we looked around to realize we were the last ones to leave.

We all climbed into our car and as the seatbelts clicked into place, I heard my husband groaning. The steering column was locked up. No turning, no way to even get the key turned in the lock. Stiff as a corpse.

Bethany asked, "What's wrong, Daddy?" After a few more unsuccessful tugs and much grunting, Todd banged his fist on the steering wheel. "The stinking wheel is locked up! We can't leave!"

The children began to worry and protest. "But how will we get home?" "Will we have to walk?" "What if a monster gets us if we walk home?" "I'm hungry and we don't have any food in here!" Yes, this brought much catastrophe to their little imaginations. I groaned inwardly, picturing having to call church members and beg one of them to come help us. The kids were already getting tired and cranky. And my husband was beginning to sound like Yosemite Sam.

My brain scrambled for an answer. My husband's frustrated tone cut through my dramatic musings. "Well, that's it! There is no way this thing is going anywhere tonight." He sighed and ran his hand through his hair. Before I even realized I was thinking it, I blurted out, "Well, of course it won't work. We haven't prayed yet!"

The girls looked at me wide-eyed, but as I bowed my head, they followed suit. "Dear Lord," I prayed, "we thank you for this car. Please help it to start tonight. We need to get home and You have the power to fix this. We will praise You for it." To add extra good measure, I laid my hands on the steering wheel. I confess, my husband looked at me like I had grown an extra head, but I forged ahead. The girls chimed in with "Jesus, I don't want to walk home!" and "Please fix the cah, Jesus...and don't let any monstuhs get us...."

In my head, I was thinking, *"Okay, Lord, the frozen car is bad enough, but now I've called upon Your help in front of my kids, showing absolute faith that you will fix this. If you don't, well...well, this may stay in their memories forever. I want them to believe that You are who You say You are. So don't leave me hanging!"*

Taking a deep breath, Todd inserted the key and tried again. Nothing.

My heart began to sink. I suggested, "Let's switch. I'll mess with it for a few minutes while you take my seat." I slid behind the wheel, silently praying, *"This is sooo not funny!"* I inserted the key. *"The girls are watching all this go down, Lord, and*

You're bailing on me here..." I turned the key and jumped when the motor roared to life. After a moment of quiet in the car, the girls began squealing and jumping up and down. "Yay! Mommy fixed it! Go, Mommy!"

"No!", I snapped, "It wasn't me! It was Jesus! We prayed and He helped us." The smiles that lit the girls' faces was priceless. They sang God's praises all the way home as Todd looked stunned and I offered my own grateful praise to our King.

We've all heard it said that there is power in prayer. In fact, I think we've heard it so much that we tend to think of it in a cliché, Christian fashion; like a droning or buzzing in our ears that we acknowledge, but have gotten so used to, it's strength has been lost.

The truth is that most of us tend to call on the Lord during the big stuff, but how much different our lives would be if we called on Him for the small stuff too! He doesn't just want to show His power to massive crowds in majestic ways, but amid the family of four who need a simple ride home.

I'm pretty sure my kids will never forget that moment, as small as it was. Pray with your spouse. Pray with your children. Pray with your parents. Pray alone in secret with our Savior.

People are watching you...and not just you, but the God you serve. Let them see His power in action.

~ ~ ~

So we've looked at the need to surrender our wounds, to embrace grace and how to know God more intimately.

Jesus is the Great Physician. The ultimate Healer. He can heal you from the damage of these landmines. He can give you the tools you need to live in joy. Let Him search Your heart. Sit at His feet. Learn His heart. Let Him be your everything.

"Then shall your light break forth like the dawn, and your healing shall spring up speedily; your righteousness shall go before you; the glory of the Lord shall be your rear guard. Then you shall call, and the Lord will answer; you shall cry, and he will say,
'Here I am.'"

~Isaiah 58:8,9

Conclusion: Dancing in Victory

Thank you so much for taking this journey with me as we've looked at the landmines that destroy our joy, unearthed their possible causes, and discovered ways to disarm them.

Remember that depression, grief, people-pleasing, perfection and anxiety are only a few of the landmines the enemy plants to destroy God's children. We are in a spiritual war, a battle that rages during every single tick of time's clock. But we don't have to stay wounded and shattered from these explosions.

And despite our pasts and our wounds, if we know Jesus, we really do have the victory: victory over death, victory over our own emotions and struggles, victory over sin. We are going to have hard times, difficult people we'd love to strangle and we still have to deal with sin. These wounds we each carry will never be completely healed until we receive our glorified bodies in heaven. But the key for now is be proactive; to learn to live in the freedom He's given. "Work out your salvation with fear and trembling..." (Philippians 12:2). We have to work these issues out; not shove them under the rug and pretend like they aren't there. Which is the whole problem with a landmine, right?

We've learned that sometimes we let our lives revolve around obeying rules, 'shoulds', pleasing people, and being 'nice'. We go through our list of things 'to do', thinking we are living in victory but later realize that those busy activities are not what God had in mind for us in the first place. The truly victorious person is just passionately in love with Jesus. He is the only thing that matters.

Don't stay in bondage when Jesus so desperately wants you to taste His goodness. Have you read the old story of the old man and the slave? It goes something like this:

A wealthy man, a southern land owner went to a slave market. Upon arriving, he noticed a young African-American man being auctioned off to the highest bidder. He bid on the young man and won. The land-owner noticed the anger glowering in the slave's dark eyes. No doubt the young man wondered how badly he would be abused at the hands of this new owner.

As the wealthy man walked off with his new 'slave', he turned to the young man and said, "You're free."

The slave looked at him in surprise. "What? What do you mean?"

"I said that you're free."

Puzzling by this unexpected announcement, the young man's eyebrows furrowed in confusion. "Does that mean I can say and do whatever I want?"

The land owner smiled. "Yes, of course."

"Can I be whatever I want to be?"

"Yes."

"Can I go wherever I want to go?"

Smiling again, the older man replied, "Of course."

Tears began to fill the young man's dark eyes. "Then I think I'll go with you."

Isn't that a beautiful picture of Christ? He bought us with an invaluably high price. And once He bought us, He set us free. Who better to stay with than the One who loved us enough to give us a choice!

God loves you, wounds and all. And no story demonstrates this quite as well as the fable of the Cracked Pots.

Cracked Pots

Indian Fable

A water bearer in India had two large pots, one hung on each end of a pole which he carried across his neck. One of the pots had a crack in it, while the other pot was perfect and always delivered a full portion of water at the end of the long walk from the stream to the master's house. The cracked pot arrived only half full.

For a full two years this went on daily, with the bearer delivering only one and half pots full of water in his master's house. Of course, the perfect pot was proud of its accomplishments, perfectly performing the job for which it was made. But the poor cracked pot was ashamed of its own imperfection, and miserable that it was able to accomplish only half of what it had been made to do.

After two years of what it perceived to be a bitter failure, it spoke to the water bearer one day by the stream. "I am ashamed of myself, and I want to apologize to you." "Why?" asked the bearer. "What are you ashamed of?"

"I have been able, for these past two years, to deliver only half my load because this crack in my side causes water to leak out all the way back to your master's house. Because of my flaws, you have to do all of this work, and you don't get full value from your efforts," the pot said.

The water bearer felt sorry for the old cracked pot, and in his compassion he said, "As we return to the master's house, I want you to notice what grows along the path back home."

As they went up the hill, the old cracked pot took notice of the sun warming the beautiful wild flowers on one side of the path. The bearer said to the pot, "Did you notice that there were flowers only on your side of the path, but not on the other pot's side? That's because I have always known about your flaw, and I took advantage of it. I planted flower seeds on your side of the path, and every day while we walk back from the stream, you've watered them." The bearer smiled and said, "Without you being the way you are, we wouldn't have the beauty you see now."

We are all cracked pots, but praise God, He still uses us for His honor, glory and plans.

My Prayer for You

Steve Brown declares "I believe the prayer God almost always answers for Christians is this: 'Lord, show me myself.' Let me tell you how God answers that prayer: *He shows you how much you are loved.* He shows you his love---a love that is absolute, unconditional, and without any requirement that you do anything to justify that love."

I pray that God will 'show you yourself' through His beautiful eyes. He's crazy about you. He'll never leave you. In seeing yourself in His eyes, I think you'll find the freedom you've been craving.

Instead of limping along, wounded and broken, you'll be running and dancing in victory.

You are loved.

APPENDIX: FIRST THINGS FIRST

Nothing in this book will make a lick of sense unless you first understand some very fundamental things. Have you wondered what it means to be a 'believer' or to be 'saved'? Let's take a look...

What do you think happens when you die?

Some of you might say, "I don't know". Some might say, "Well, I'm basically a good person, so I guess I'll go to heaven."

Let's look at that for a moment.

Let's go through the Ten Commandments and see how good you are. (Exodus 20) Have you ever told a lie? If the answer is yes, that means you are a liar. I know, I know...putting it so bluntly hurts. But we are trying to be honest here. How many lies do you think you have told during your entire life?

Have you ever wanted something that wasn't yours? That is called coveting...and it's a sin. Have you ever been disrespectful to your parents? Have you ever thought about being with someone who wasn't your spouse? Have you ever cursed using God's name?

See, the problem is that if you have done any of these things, that means you are a sinner. (And I haven't even mentioned about five of the other commandments.) Sin means to 'fall short of the mark'. To make a mistake. And guess what? We've all done it! *"For all have sinned and fall short of the glory of God."* ~Romans 3:23

Compared to God's holiness, His absolute perfection, we all have messed up. It's easy to compare ourselves to others and say, "well, at least I'm not like so-and-so". But comparing ourselves to another person really isn't the best standard is it?

I'll put it this way. My little bichon dog is adorable with big black eyes and fluffy white fur. Inside of our house, she looks pristinely white. Perfect. But the last time it snowed, she ran outside all excited and I was startled to watch her playing in the snow. She looked dirty! And dingy and yellow.

That's how we arecompared to God. Dirty, dingy...unclean.

Now, you may stop here and say, "Okay, I'm not perfect but I've done some good things in my life." Consider what would happen if a murderer stood before a judge. He is waiting for sentencing after admitting that he has killed. Yet he stands before the judge and says, 'I admit I've killed, but you're not taking the balance into account. I've been nice to people in the past and I've given to charity." What would the judge say?

A good judge would never let a criminal go just because he had done some good things in the past. He would judge according to the crime committed, because a good judge must uphold justice. And God is a good judge. *"For the wages of sin is death..."* ~Romans 6:23

So knowing that we all sin, where do we deserve to go? To heaven or hell?

To hell. I deserve to go there but God loved us...he loved *you* so much, that He provided a way.

He sent His only Son Jesus to earth. Jesus compressed himself into the womb of a virgin, was born in Bethlehem, grew into a young man. He was God wrapped in human flesh. And being God, He showed His power by healing the sick, raising the dead and teaching us about God's love.

Jesus never sinned. *"For we do not have a high priest who is unable to empathize with our weaknesses, but we have one who has been tempted in every way, just as we are—yet he did not sin."* (Hebrews 4:15) Jesus loves us and cares so deeply for us that He refused to leave us in the dark. At the age of 33, He allowed an angry mob that feared losing their power to beat him, spit on him, be whipped with a cat-of-nine-tails and be crucified to a Roman cross. At that moment, He took all of our sin, our mistakes on Himself and nailed them to His cross. Simply put, He took the whipping for every bad thing you and I have ever done and ever will do.

Now, if Jesus is dead, what good does it do? But praise God, He's *not* dead! Three days after dying, He was raised from the dead and appeared to hundreds of witnesses. (Study the book of John to learn more.) When He rose from the dead, it means He conquered death and sin....forever.

Now, is it enough to believe that there is a God? No. James 2:19 says, *"You believe that there is one God. Good! Even the demons believe that—and tremble."* If you want to be clean, to stand before God the judge blameless and perfect, you need to ask Jesus to forgive you and to save you from an eternal hell. *"If you declare with your mouth, 'Jesus is Lord,' and believe in your heart that God raised him from the dead, you will be saved. For it is with your heart that you believe and are justified, and it is with your mouth that you profess your faith and are saved."* (Romans 10:9-10)

Since the moment I asked God to forgive me and claimed Jesus as my King, my life has never been the same. He gives peace when everything is crashing around me. He loves me when I feel unlovable. And He is building a home for me in

Heaven as we speak. He has transformed me from a person who was dead inside to a new creation in Him.

Will you give your life to Him today?

REFERENCES

Brown, Steve. *A Scandalous Freedom: The Radical Nature of the Gospel.* West Monroe, LA: Howard Publishing Co., Inc., 2004.

Cloud, Henry & Townsend, John. *Boundaries: When to Say Yes, When to Say No To Take Control of Your Life.* Grand Rapids, Michigan: Zondervan, 1992.

Cloud, Henry. *Changes that Heal.* Grand Rapids, Michigan: Zondervan, 1990.

Cloud, Henry & Townsend, John. *Safe People: How to Find Relationships That are Good for You And Avoid Those That Aren't.* Grand Rapids, Michigan: Zondervan, 1995.

Comfort, Ray. *Overcoming Panic Attacks.* Alachua, FL: Bridge-Logos, 2005.

Crabb, Larry. *Inside Out.* Colorado Springs, CO: NavPress, 1988.

Crosby, Fannie. *Fannie Crosby: An Autobiography.* Peabody, Massachusetts: Hendrickson Publishers, Inc., 2008.

Hall, Mark. *Stained Glass Masquerade* from the album *Lifesong* by Casting Crowns. Reunion Records, 2005.

Hawkins, Tim. *Full Range of Motion* (DVD). Tunafish Productions LP, 2006. www.timhawkins.net

Jones, Brian. *Overcoming Grief.* People of Faith, 2004. http://www.peopleoffaith.com/overcoming-grief.htm

Lucado, Max. *It's Not About Me, Teen Edition.* Nashville, TN: Thomas Nelson, Inc., 2005.

Miller, Donald. *Blue Like Jazz.* Nashville, TN: Thomas Nelson, Inc., 2003.

Miller, Donald. *Searching for God Knows What.* Nashville, TN: Thomas Nelson, Inc., 2004.

Moore, Beth. *David: Seeking a Heart Like His.* Nashville, TN: LifeWay Press, 2010.

Moore, Beth. *James: Mercy Triumphs.* Nashville, TN: LifeWay Press, 2011.

Murphy, Richard A. *Statistics About Pastors.* Maranatha Life, 2002. http://maranathalife.com/lifeline/stats.htm

Ranier, Thomas. *When Pastors Experience Depression.* The Christian Post, 2001. http://www.christianpost.com/news/when-pastors-experience-depression-52553/

Ten Boom, Corrie and Buckingham, Jamie. *Tramp for the Lord.* Fort Washington, PA: CLC Publications, 1974

Townsend, John. *Where is God?* Nashville, TN: Thomas Nelson, Inc., 2009.

Warner, Greg. *Suicide: When Pastors' Silent Suffering Turns Tragic.* USA Today, 2009. http://www.usatoday30.usatoday.com/news/religion/2009-10-28-pastor_suicides_N.htm

Hollow Victory · 255

About the Author

Tara Johnson is a singer, songwriter and author. In 2004, she signed with Incubator Creative Group, a ministry management label based in Eugene, Oregon. Tara's ministry is built on helping those struggling with depression, people-pleasing and grief, through stories, music, comedy and writing.

Several of Tara's articles have been published in *Plain Truth Magazine* and in 2012, she won a bronze medal in The Frasier awards, hosted by My Book Therapy.

She and her husband make their home in the beautiful state of Arkansas and have been blessed with five beautiful children, two of which are in heaven: Bethany, Callie, Taylor, Morgan and Nathan.

Tara loves to connect with her readers. You can meet her and find other helpful resources to grow on your spiritual journey at the contact points below:

Tara@TaraJohnsonMinistries.com
Twitter @TaraMinistry
www.TaraJohnsonMinistries.com
www.Facebook.com/tara.johnson.1401

c/o Incubator Creative Group
Post Office Box 245
Cheshire, OR 97419
www.IncubatorOnline.com

Made in the USA
San Bernardino, CA
17 March 2014